EASY and FUN
Christmas Quilts

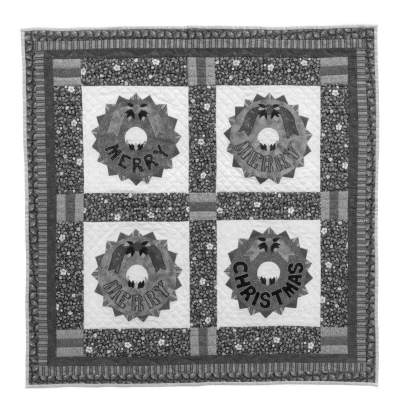

EILEEN WESTFALL

Martingale
& COMPANY

Bothell, Washington

DEDICATION

To my dear son, Damian Drew.

"Children are a gift from the Lord."
Psalms 127:3

I am thankful for you in my life!

ACKNOWLEDGMENTS

**Thanks and gratitude to my quilting friends
who helped me make the quilts in this book—
Katherine Bilton, Gwen Boreo, Kim Chan,
Diana Near, Donna Remorini,
and Anna Stoltzfus.**

That Patchwork Place is an imprint of
Martingale & Company.

Easy and Fun Christmas Quilts
© 2000 by Eileen Westfall

Martingale & Company
PO Box 118
Bothell, WA 98041-0118 USA
www.patchwork.com

Printed in China
05 04 03 02 01 00   6 5 4 3 2 1

Credits

President . . . . Nancy J. Martin
CEO . . . . Daniel J. Martin
Publisher . . . . Jane Hamada
Editorial Director . . . . Mary V. Green
Technical Editor . . . . Ursula Reikes
Copy Editor . . . . Ellen Balstad
Design and Production Manager . . . . Stan Green
Illustrator . . . . Laurel Strand
Photographer . . . . Brent Kane
Text Designer . . . . Kay Green
Cover Designer . . . . Stan Green

Library of Congress Cataloging-in-Publication Data

Westfall, Eileen.
    Easy and fun Christmas quilts/Eileen Westfall.
        p. cm.
    ISBN 1-56477-301-9
        1. Patchwork—Patterns. 2. Appliqué—Patterns.
    3. Christmas decorations. 4. Miniature quilts. I. Title.
    TT835.W485 2000
    746.46'041—dc21   00-026003

MISSION STATEMENT

*We are dedicated to providing quality
products and service by working together
to inspire creativity and to enrich
the lives we touch.*

Contents

 *Introduction*

People have always referred to me as a "Christmas nut." When I hear people grumbling that the department stores have their Christmas displays up too early, I wonder what they are talking about. It's never too early! I love to see the new ornaments, the decorations, and the trees for the coming holiday—I love anything that makes Christmas special. Each year I start decorating the day after Thanksgiving. I believe that the entire month of December should be a Christmas celebration. I put away my usual decorations, which include quilts on most of the walls, and put up everything related to Christmas.

When I started designing quilts in 1981, the majority of my ideas were for Christmas quilts. In fact, the first book I wrote was *A Patchwork Christmas* in 1985. Since then, I have written many books on various subjects, but I have longed to do another Christmas book.

When I began to think about and gather designs for this book, I wanted Christmas designs that someone could make quickly. Once I started, ideas just seemed to pop into my head. I also searched through my "idea" file and found several more. One design, "Candles for Christmas," had been lingering in my thoughts for years until now. I also adapted part of a pattern given to me by my first quilt teacher many years ago to create "Dutch Treat." Before I knew it, I had fourteen designs on paper.

The idea behind the designs in this book was that someone could make a friend a quick gift if the time to make the quilt could be condensed. (As you will see, the directions for all of the projects are written for quick and easy fusible appliqué, but you can also appliqué the designs by hand; it all depends on your time.)

It took me about ten months, with the help of several friends, to make all the quilts for this book. As each one was finished, it was exciting to see the colored sketch transformed into a quilt. I also enjoyed selecting the holiday fabrics and seeing how they looked when they were sewn together.

Having completed the fourteen samples, what I am doing right now? I'm working on a new Christmas quilt! You see, I never stop thinking about Christmas. I hope you are inspired to make these quilts to give as gifts or to keep for yourself to decorate your home.

Eileen Westfall

Quiltmaking Basics

All projects in this book include a list of supplies, a cutting guide, and complete directions. Measurements are provided for pieces that can be cut using a rotary cutter, and full-size templates are included for pieces that will be fused.

Yardage requirements are based on fabric that is at least 42" wide after prewashing. If your fabric is narrower than 42", you may have to adjust the amounts listed in the quilt plans.

SUPPLIES

For best results, you need to have some good basic equipment. This section lists everything you need to make the projects.

Sewing Machine

You will need a sewing machine to make the projects in this book. Make sure it is in good working order before you begin sewing. I own an inexpensive, no-frills machine that makes only straight or zigzag stitches. It's a great sewing machine and does all I need to do for my quilting projects.

Needles and Pins

Start each project with a new sewing-machine needle. Use a size 70/10 or 80/12 needle for cotton fabrics.

Use silk pins or ball-tip pins with round, colored heads for pinning pieces together prior to stitching. They are sharp and glide through the fabric smoothly, and you can find them easily.

You will need embroidery needles for the quilts that feature some embroidery. Look for packages that contain an assortment of embroidery needles. Quilting needles are essential if you're going to hand quilt. A package of quilting needles, or Betweens, may contain an assortment of needle sizes from size 7 to size 12. The higher the number, the finer and shorter the needle. Despite seeming difficult to handle at first, a smaller needle makes it easier to make tiny stitches.

Thread

I learned an important lesson from my first quilt project: always use sewing thread that matches the fabric, or is at least close in color value. Some suggestions for colors to use include off-white, tan, and light gray for light fabrics, or navy blue, black, and dark gray for darker fabrics.

Rotary Cutter

Rotary cutters are available in a variety of sizes and are made by several different manufacturers. The cutter features a very sharp, circular blade. Before cutting, visually check the path the blade will take to make sure that your fingers are not in the way. Always cut away from your body and close the safety shield when the cutter is not in use.

Replace the blades when they become dull. Keep extra blades on hand to prevent the frustration of cutting with a dull or nicked blade. It's also a good idea to clean your cutter each time you start a new project. Take the cutter apart and wipe the blade with a soft cloth. Reassemble the cutter and place a drop of sewing-machine oil between the blade and the safety shield.

Rotary-Cutting Mat

Rotary-cutting mats come in many different sizes. They are made from a material that is impervious to the cuts of a rotary cutter and should last for years. A mat printed with a 1" grid will make cutting easier and more accurate. Look for one that has ⅛" measurements along the outer grid and diagonal lines to help when cutting bias strips.

 **TIP**

Never leave your rotary-cutting mat in the car on a hot day. It will buckle from the heat and be unusable.

Rulers

You will also need special rulers that have inches marked both vertically and horizontally. I recommend a 3" x 18" ruler, a 6" x 24" ruler, and a 6" Bias Square® ruler. Visit your local quilt shop to see what other rulers are available.

Scissors

Keep a separate pair of scissors just for fabric and be sure they are sharp. Use another pair for cutting paper and template plastic.

Seam Ripper

Use a seam ripper to reduce the frustration of removing a seam. Slip the point of the seam ripper under a stitch, pushing forward and pulling up to break the thread. Work along the seam, breaking every third or fourth stitch. At the end of the seam, carefully pull the two pieces of fabric apart. They should separate easily. Remove the bits of thread and restitch the seam.

Marking Tools

Erasable marking pens are available with two different kinds of ink: one fades with time and the other washes out with water. Each one has advantages and disadvantages.

Fading-ink pens make light marks that may fade before a project is completed, which means you may need to mark the project again. I use fading-ink markers only on small pieces that I know I can complete quickly. The ink that washes out with water is usually a brighter color than the ink that fades; however, traces of the ink may reappear after drying. Fabric may have to be washed many times before the markings disappear completely.

Other markers you might want to try include a pencil that erases easily and chalk in stick form. Ask at your local quilt store for these and other marking tools.

Masking Tape

Marking straight lines is easy with masking tape. It is available in various widths at the hardware store, but ¼"-wide tape is the most convenient for quilting. Look for ¼"-wide quilter's tape at your local quilt shop.

Apply the tape to the top of the quilt as a guide, and stitch on either side of the tape. Don't leave the tape on your quilt for an extended period of time because it can leave a residue that is difficult to remove.

Thimbles

I have a confession to make. In the many years I have been sewing, I have never felt comfortable using a thimble. I am left-handed, and I do many things upside-down or backward, which could be the source of what I call "thimble block." Do yourself a favor and use a thimble if you can. A thimble protects your fingers and pushes the needle more easily though the fabric. You will enjoy painless sewing and quilting.

FABRIC

Many people love to collect fabric so that they will have some on hand when a creative idea strikes them. I keep fabric scraps in color-keyed, resealable plastic bags in a box for small projects. When I am looking for the right color of fabric, I can usually find what I need without making a trip to the fabric store. I think it's fun to keep scraps of truly wonderful fabric and a challenge to use them in a second and even a third project. As you will find in this book, several of the projects can be made with scraps of fabric.

I recommend 100 percent cotton for all your quilting projects. Polyester and polyester blends pucker and pull, and they don't give the fine results that all-cotton fabrics do. Always check the end of the fabric bolt to be certain of the fabric content when you purchase your material.

Wash all fabric before beginning a project. Eliminate shrinkage before cutting and stitching, not after a project is completed. Press your fabric in preparation for cutting, using a steam iron to remove wrinkles.

Fabric is made with threads (called yarns) that are woven together at right angles. The lengthwise grain runs parallel to the selvage and has little stretch, while the crosswise grain runs from selvage to selvage and has some stretch. These threads are considered the straight grain. Cut pieces on either the lengthwise or crosswise grain of the fabric unless otherwise instructed.

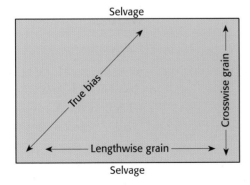

Cuts made on the diagonal are considered bias. A true bias runs at a 45° angle to the lengthwise and crosswise grains and has the most stretch.

ROTARY CUTTING

All the patchwork pieces in this book can be cut using a rotary cutter. Patterns are provided for appliqué designs. If you are new to rotary cutting, take a class at your local quilt shop or fabric store to learn how to use a rotary cutter. The following steps also describe the process.

1. Lay the fabric on a cutting mat, with the folded edge toward you and the selvages away from you. Align the folded edge with a horizontal line.

2. Align the edge of a Bias Square ruler on the bottom fold of the fabric. Place a long ruler to the left, slightly beyond the left raw edge, so it is flush with the Bias Square. Remove the Bias Square and cut the fabric from the fold to the top edge.

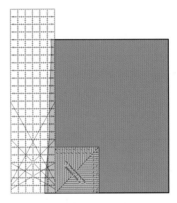

3. To cut a strip, align the desired measurement of the long ruler with the just-cut edge of the fabric. For example, to cut a 2½"-wide strip, place the 2½" ruler mark on the edge of the fabric.

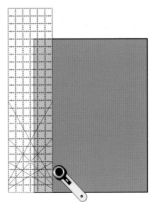

Cutting Squares and Rectangles

To cut squares, start by cutting a strip in the required size. For example, if you need 3½" squares, cut a 3½"-wide strip. Place the strip on the mat lengthwise and trim the selvages. Align the 3½" marks on the Bias Square with the left edge and bottom edge of the strip. Cut along the right side of the ruler. Continue across the strip, working from left to right, until you have the required number of squares.

To cut rectangles, follow the same procedure but make the second cut the length of the required rectangle.

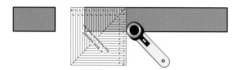

Cutting Half-Square Triangles

Cut squares once diagonally to create triangles with the straight of grain on the two short sides. To account for seam allowances, cut squares ⅞" larger than the desired finished size of the short edge of the triangles.

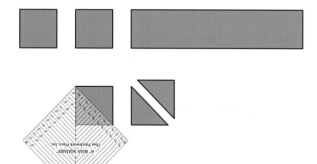

Cutting Quarter-Square Triangles

Cut a square twice diagonally to create triangles with the straight of grain on the long edges. To account for seam allowances, cut squares 1¼" larger than the desired finished size of the long edge of the triangles.

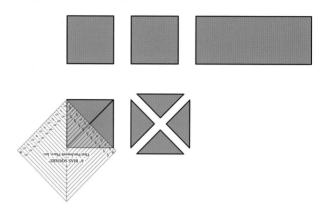

PIECING TIPS

Accuracy is of the utmost importance in patchwork, and precise cutting is at the heart of that accuracy. It requires special care in preparing the fabric and in the actual cutting. These tips will help you make your quilting more accurate and easier to do.

Check Your Stitch Length

Set your sewing machine for short stitches—about twelve per inch. Long, loose stitches can come undone. Small stitches are strong stitches.

Stitch Uniform Seams

All of the patchwork projects in this book require ¼"-wide seam allowances. Varia- 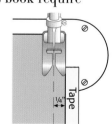 tions in your seam width will distort the shape of the project and make assembling the pieces and blocks frustrating. If your sewing machine doesn't have a ¼" guide, place a piece of tape ¼" from the needle to use as a guide.

Pressing

After stitching pieces, strips, or blocks, press seam allowances toward the darker fabric whenever possible. This prevents darker seam allowances from showing though lighter fabrics on the front of the project.

When joining rows of blocks or pairs of pieces, press the seam allowances in opposite directions from row to row. When you pin the rows together, the seam allowances will butt up against each other and create a firm fit.

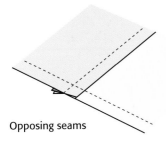

Opposing seams

FUSIBLE APPLIQUÉ

Fusible appliqué is fast and fun. It requires the use of a paper-backed fusible web product, which is ironed to the wrong side of the fabric. Shapes can then be cut from the fused fabric and ironed to a background fabric.

There are many brands of fusible webbing available. Look for a lightweight, paper-backed fusible web. The bonded fabric should be soft and subtle after fusing so that you can embroider and quilt through it if desired. If you're not sure of which webbing to choose, ask the salesperson to recommend one for the type of projects you're doing.

The patterns for fusible appliqué in this book are reversed from the way they appear in the finished design. See the note on page 10 if you intend to hand appliqué the designs.

1. Trace each appliqué shape onto the paper side of the fusible web. See sidebar below for information about cutting pieces that are underneath other pieces. Cut out the shape, leaving a ¼" margin all around.

Many appliqué shapes overlap other shapes. Be sure to trace each shape separately, adding a little extra on the portion of any appliqué piece that will be underneath another piece. In the following example, a dashed line indicates where to draw the line for pieces 1, 2, and 3.

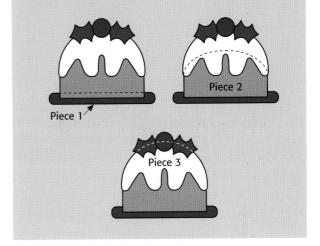

Piece 1

Piece 2

Piece 3

2. Fuse the shape to the wrong side of the fabric.

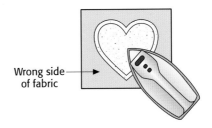

Wrong side of fabric

3. Cut out the shape exactly on the traced line.

4. Remove the paper. Lay the fabric shape on the background fabric, fusible web side down. Following the manufacturer's directions, press in place.

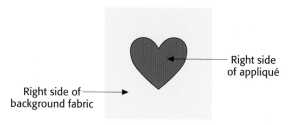

Right side of appliqué

Right side of background fabric

If you accidentally fuse a piece of fabric to the wrong place, remove the piece immediately. If any glue remains on the background fabric, put a little water (from a spray bottle) on it and use your fingernail to scratch the glue off the fabric. Once you've removed all the glue, press the fabric.

NOTE: *If you prefer to hand appliqué the designs, you will need to reverse the patterns; otherwise, your design will be a mirror image of the finished design. Trace the patterns onto template plastic and cut them out. Label each template with the piece number and pattern. Place the right side of the plastic template on the right side of the fabric and trace around it with a marking pen or pencil. Cut out the shapes, adding a ¼" seam allowance beyond the traced line.*

EMBROIDERY STITCHES

All the projects in this book require some embroidery. Use the embroidery stitches shown below. The number of strands to use is indicated in the quilt directions.

When working with the appliqué pieces, you will need to trace the embroidery patterns before you fuse the appliqué pieces in place. However, you have the option of doing the embroidery work

either before or after fusing. Look for a lightweight, flexible, fusible web. If your fusible web is stiff, it may be difficult to embroider after fusing.

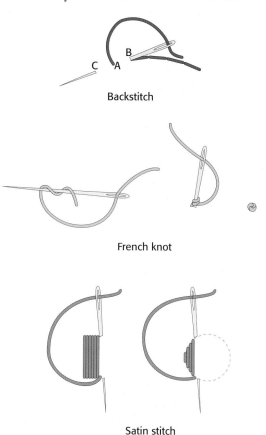

Backstitch

French knot

Satin stitch

FINISHING

Batting

Batting comes in various weights, but I prefer lightweight batting—especially for the wall quilts in this book. Lightweight batting makes it easier to quilt through the three quilt layers and will not give you a puffy effect.

You can purchase batting in two forms: prepackaged or by the yard. Batting on a roll is often 60" and is usually less expensive than prepackaged batting. Cut the batting 4" larger than the quilt top all around. During the quilting process, the batting may pull in a little, so it's best to have a little extra.

Backing

All of the projects in this book are small enough that backing can be made without piecing. However, you may want to be creative and piece or appliqué designs on your quilt backing just for fun. Be sure to cut the fabric for the backing 3" larger that the quilt top on all four sides.

Layering the Quilt

The quilt sandwich consists of three layers—the backing, the batting, and the quilt top. Mark the quilt top with any quilting designs before layering the quilt (see page 12).

1. Place the backing, wrong side up, on a large table. Use masking tape to anchor the backing to the table, making sure it's flat and wrinkle free.
2. Place the batting on top of the backing, smoothing out all the wrinkles.
3. Place the pressed quilt top on top of the batting. Smooth out any wrinkles and make sure the edges of the quilt top are parallel to the edges of the backing.
4. Baste with needle and thread or safety pins as described below.

Basting

Basting is time consuming, but it ensures that your quilt will lie flat and smooth. There are two methods of basting: with a needle and thread or with safety pins.

Needle and Thread

Use a regular sewing needle and light-colored thread. (Dark-colored thread may bleed onto the quilt.). Beginning at the center of the quilt, baste the layers together with long running stitches in horizontal rows about 6" to 8" apart. Then stitch in vertical rows, also 6" to 8" apart, until the whole quilt is basted. Add a row of basting around

the outside edges. Do not remove the basting stitches until the entire project is quilted.

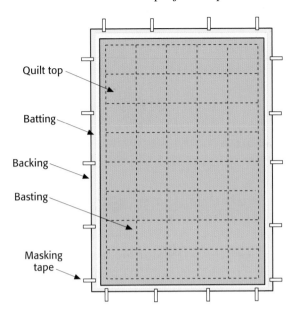

Safety Pins

This is a fast and easy way of basting. Use rust-proof, size 2 safety pins. Begin pinning in the center and work toward the outside edges. Work in horizontal rows, placing pins about 4" to 6" apart. With a needle and thread, add a row of basting stitches around the outside edges of the quilt.

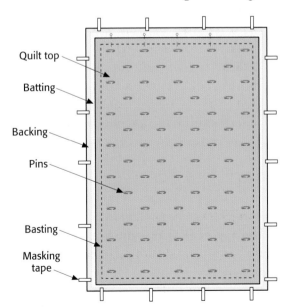

Quilting

Marking

Marking the quilt top is important because the lines you mark will be your quilting guide. You will need to mark quilting motifs and complex quilting designs before layering the quilt. It is not necessary to mark lines if you will be outline quilting, quilting in the ditch or doing other straight-line quilting. Use quilter's ¼" tape to keep lines straight. For marking small quilts and wall hangings, I recommend using either a light box or a window.

Light Box

Place the design on a light box and turn the light on. Position the quilt top at the desired point and trace the design with a marking pen. Move the design and quilt top as needed to complete the design.

You can create a makeshift light box by pulling apart your dining table and placing a piece of glass or Plexiglas over the gap. A lighted lamp on the floor beneath the table provides the light.

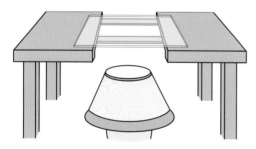

Make your own light box.

Window

You can also use the light from a window to illuminate the design you want to trace. Tape the design to a window. Place the quilt top over the design and use a removable marking pen to mark the design. Move the design and quilt top as needed to complete the design.

Frames and Hoops

For large quilts some quilters use a quilting frame. For the small quilts in this book, use a quilting hoop. A quilting hoop is heavier than an embroidery hoop and may come with an attached stand.

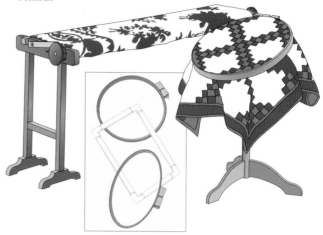

Quilting Styles

All the projects in this book were quilted by hand. Complete quilting diagrams are not included; however, you can purchase templates at your local quilt store and apply whatever motif or design you choose to the quilt.

The four quilting styles used on these quilts are

- Single outline quilting, which consists of one line of stitching ¼" from the seam lines of the patchwork pieces.
- Double outline quilting, which consists of two lines of stitching that follow the seam lines. The first line is ¼" from the seam and the second is ¼" from the first line.
- Quilting in the ditch, which involves stitching on the side of seams that don't have the seam allowance. The stitches may not be visible, but the indent of the quilting stands out.
- Motif quilting, which involves quilting a design, usually in an unpieced area such as the border or the center of a block.

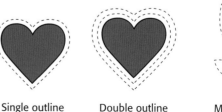

Single outline quilting   Double outline quilting   Motif quilting

Quilting Stitch

Quilting consists of short running stitches through three layers—the backing, the batting, and the quilt top. Use the smallest Between needle you can comfortably handle. The smaller the needle, the smaller the stitches.

1. Thread needle with an 18"-long strand of quilting thread. Make a knot in one end.
2. Push the needle from the back through the quilt top about 1" from where your quilting line will begin. Push the needle out about 1" from where the stitching will be and gently pull the thread until the knot pops through the fabric into the batting.
3. Take small, even stitches through all 3 layers, rocking the needle up and down and taking 3 or more stitches on the needle at a time.
4. To end a line of quilting, make a small knot close to the last stitch on the backside; then take a backstitch through the quilt top and bring the needle up a needle's length away. Pull the thread until the knot pops into the batting and carefully clip the thread.

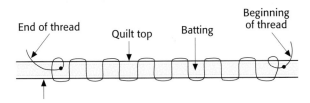

End of thread   Quilt top   Batting   Beginning of thread

❖ TIP ❖

I have heard of many people taking a nick out of their quilt while they were cutting thread. To avoid this, try this tip that my first quilting teacher gave me. Hold a pair of scissors open and lean it on the thread. If the scissors are sharp enough, they will cut the thread without having to do any cutting motion.

Binding

When the quilting is finished, trim the batting and backing to the same size as the quilt top in preparation for binding. Next, for straight-grain binding cut 2"-wide strips across the width of the binding fabric. You will need enough binding to go around the perimeter of the quilt plus 10" for turning the corners and overlapping the ends.

To attach the binding, follow these steps:

1. Stitch the strips together, offsetting them as shown. Trim seam allowances to ¼". Press the seams open.

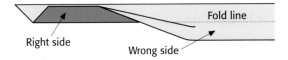

2. Cut one end of strip at a 45° angle. Fold the strip in half lengthwise, wrong sides together, and press.

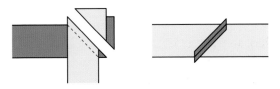

Right side   Fold line   Wrong side

3. Unfold the binding strip at the angled end and turn under ¼".

Fold line

4. Beginning on a side of the quilt and aligning the raw edges of the strip with the raw edges of the quilt, stitch the binding strip to the quilt. Use a ¼"-wide seam allowance. Start stitching 1" to 2" from the start of the binding. Stop stitching ¼" from the first corner and backstitch.

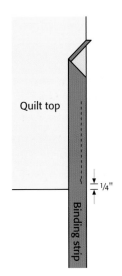

Quilt top

¼"

Binding strip

5. Turn the quilt to prepare for sewing along the next edge. Fold the binding away from the quilt; then fold again to place the binding along the second edge of the quilt. This fold creates an angled pleat at the corner.

6. Stitch from the fold of the binding along the second edge of the quilt top. Stop ¼" from the corner as you did for the first corner; back-stitch. Repeat the stitching and mitering process on the remaining edges and corners of the quilt

7. When you reach the beginning of the binding, cut the end 1" longer than needed and tuck the end inside the beginning. Stitch the rest of the binding.

8. Turn the binding to the backside of the quilt, over the raw edges. Blindstitch the binding in place, with the folded edge covering the row of machine stitching. At each corner, fold the binding to form a miter on the back of the quilt.

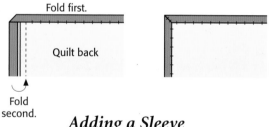

Fold first.

Quilt back

Fold second.

Adding a Sleeve

All the quilts in this book are suitable for hanging on a wall. For proper hanging, add a sleeve so you can slip a hanging rod or dowel through it.

1. Cut a strip of fabric 8" wide and ½" shorter than the finished width of your quilt.
2. Turn the strip under ¼" at both ends. Press and turn under ¼" again. Stitch by machine to finish the ends.

3. Fold the strip in half lengthwise, wrong sides together, with raw edges aligned. Stitch along the length of the strip ¼" from the raw edges.

Stitch raw edges.

4. Press the seam open, centering it on the back of the sleeve.

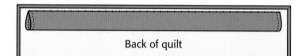

Center seam and press open.

5. Pin the tube in place just below the top inner edge of the binding. Blindstitch the top edge of the sleeve to the quilt. Be sure your stitches do not go through to the front side of the quilt.

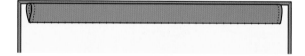

Back of quilt

Blindstitch top edge of sleeve.

6. Push the tube up just a little before blindstitching the bottom edge to the quilt. This will give enough fullness so the hanging rod or dowel will have enough room to slide comfortably through the sleeve.

Push tube up and tack down bottom edge.

Insert hanging rod or dowel in sleeve.

Making a Label

Make a label for your quilt by embroidering the name of the quilt, your name, and the date the quilt was finished on a small piece of fabric. You can also write this information on the fabric with a permanent marking pen. Appliqué the label to the back of the quilt.

Christmas Tea

Finished Quilt Size: 32" x 32"

CHRISTMAS TEA by Eileen Westfall, 1999, Walnut Creek, California. Hand quilted by Anna Stoltzfus. One Christmas our family went to England to visit a friend who had moved there. We were excited about spending the Christmas holiday—British-style—with our friend in her new surroundings. One of the highlights of that visit was going to high tea in a stately old mansion. I have never forgotten that experience and designed this quilt to capture the memory of that special time.

MATERIALS

42"-wide fabric

⅜ yd. red-and-white print for background triangles
⅔ yd. white solid for center square
⅔ yd. beige-and-white print for background triangles
½ yd. multicolored print for border
⅜ yd. for binding
Scraps of solids and prints in the following colors for appliqué: yellow, medium brown, dark brown, medium blue, and red
1 skein of embroidery floss in each of the following colors: dark green and brown
36" x 36" piece of batting
1 yd. for backing

CUTTING

From the red-and-white print, cut:
2 squares, each 8" x 8". Iron the squares onto a piece of paper-backed fusible web of the same size. Trim the squares to 7⅜" x 7⅜", and cut once diagonally to make 4 triangles (B).

From the white solid, cut:
1 square, 18½" x 18½" (A)

From the beige-and-white print, cut:
1 square, 19¼" x 19¼". Cut twice diagonally to make 4 triangles (C)

From the multicolored print, cut:
2 strips, each 3½" x 26" (D)
2 strips, each 3½" x 32" (E)

From the fabric for the binding, cut:
4 strips, each 2" x 42"

PATCHWORK

1. Fuse a red-and-white B triangle to each corner of the white A square. Join 2 beige-and-white C triangles to opposite sides of the white square. Join 2 beige-and-white C triangles to the remaining sides.

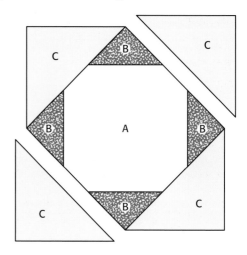

2. Add the multicolored D strips to the sides of the quilt top first; then add the multicolored E strips to the top and bottom edges.

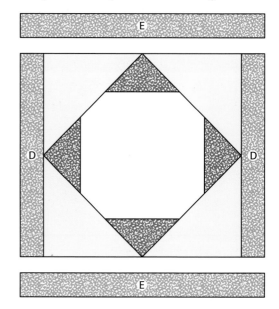

APPLIQUÉ AND EMBROIDERY

Using the patterns on pages 18–19, prepare appliqué shapes following the directions for fusible appliqué on pages 9–10. Appliqué the pieces in numerical order. Appliqué the leaves and berries in the center square after embroidering the branches.

EMBROIDER THE FOLLOWING:				
Location	**Color of Floss**	**Number of Strands**	**Stitch**	**Item to Embroider**
Center square	Dark green	4	Backstitch	Words
Center square	Brown	2	Backstitch	Branches, strings on tea bags, lines on tea bags

FINISHING

1. Layer the quilt top with batting and backing; baste. Quilt as desired.
2. Bind the edges of the quilt.
3. Add a sleeve, if desired.

Tea Pot
Cut pieces to make 4.

Border Star
Cut 8.

Sugar Bowl
Cut pieces to make 1.

Cup
Cut pieces to make 1 and 1 reversed.

Creamer
Cut pieces to make 1.

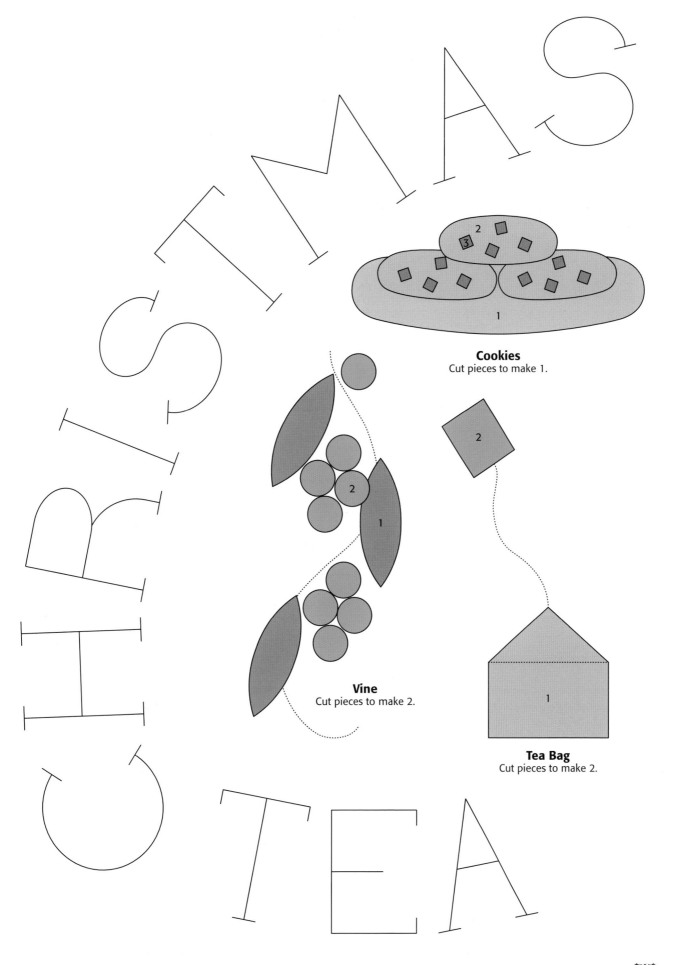

Cookies
Cut pieces to make 1.

Vine
Cut pieces to make 2.

Tea Bag
Cut pieces to make 2.

I Heard the Bells on Christmas Day

Finished Quilt Size: 29½" x 29½"

I HEARD THE BELLS ON CHRISTMAS DAY by Eileen Westfall, 1999, Walnut Creek, California. Hand quilted by Kim Chan. The inspiration for this quilt was taken from an old Christmas carol that includes these lines: "I heard the bells on Christmas Day, its old familiar carols play." Since I have no bells to ring out on Christmas, I let this quilt say "Merry Christmas" in a special way.

MATERIALS

42"-wide fabric

¼ yd. red-and-gold print for Bow blocks
½ yd. white solid for Bow blocks and center
    square
¼ yd. red-and-white check for Bow blocks
¼ yd. red-and-cream plaid for background
⅝ yd. multicolored print for border
⅜ yd. for binding
Scraps of solids and prints in the following col-
    ors for appliqué: gold, red, green, and red-
    and-white striped
1 skein of black embroidery floss
34" x 34" piece of batting
1 yd. for backing

CUTTING

From the red-and-gold print, cut:
    24 squares, each 1⅞" x 1⅞". Cut once diago-
      nally to make 48 triangles (A).
    28 squares, each 1½" x 1½" (B)

From the white solid, cut:
    36 squares, each 1⅞" x 1⅞". Cut once diago-
      nally to make 72 triangles (A).
    8 squares, each 1½" x 1½" (B)
    16 rectangles, each 1½" x 2½" (C)
    4 rectangles, each 2½" x 5½" (D)
    1 square, 7½" x 7½" (E)

From the red-and-white check, cut:
    12 squares, each 1⅞" x 1⅞". Cut once diago-
      nally to make 24 triangles (A)
    16 squares, each 1½" x 1½" (B)

From the red-and-cream plaid, cut:
    4 squares, each 7½" x 7½" (E)

From the multicolored print, cut:
    2 strips, each 4½" x 21½" (F)
    2 strips, each 4½" x 29½" (G)

From the fabric for the binding, cut:
    4 strips, each 2" x 42"

PATCHWORK

1. Join a red-and-gold A triangle and a white A
triangle to make Unit 1. Make 48 units. Join
a red-and-white A triangle and a white A triangle to make Unit 2. Make 24 units.

Unit 1
Make 48.

Unit 2
Make 24.

2. Join 4 of Unit 1, 2 red-and-gold B squares, 1
of Unit 2, 1 red-and-white B square, and 1
white B square to make each of the top left
and top right sections. Make 4 of each.

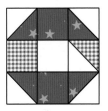

Top left section
Make 4.

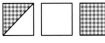

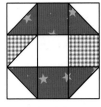

Top right section
Make 4.

3. Join 2 of Unit 1, 1 of Unit 2, 1 red-and-gold B square, and 1 white C rectangle to make each of the middle left and middle right sections. Make 4 of each section.

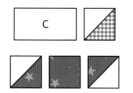

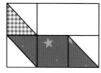

Middle left section
Make 4.

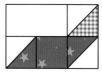

Middle right section
Make 4.

4. Join 2 of Unit 2, 2 red-and-white B squares, and 1 white D rectangle to make the bottom row.

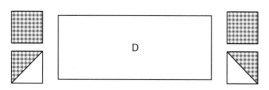

5. Join 1 white C rectangle and 1 red-and-gold B square. Sew this between a top left and a top right section to make the top row. Join 1 white C rectangle, 1 middle left section, and 1 middle right section to make the middle row. Join the top, middle, and bottom rows to complete a Bow block. Make 4 Bow blocks.

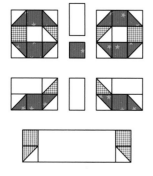

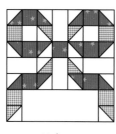

Make 4.

6. Join 1 Bow block between 2 red-and-cream E squares to make each of the top and bottom rows. Join the white E square between 2 Bow blocks to make the middle row. Join the top, middle, and bottom rows to make the center section.

7. Add the multicolored F strips to the sides of the quilt top first; then add the multicolored G strips to the top and bottom edges.

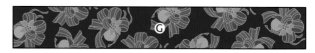

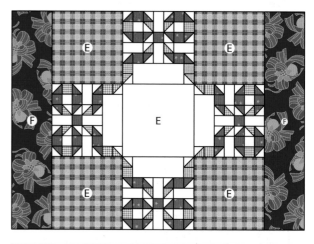

Appliqué and Embroidery

Using the patterns on pages 24–25, prepare appliqué shapes following the directions for fusible appliqué on pages 9–10. Appliqué the pieces in numerical order. To make three-dimensional mistletoe berries, sew a running stitch around the edge of the circle. Pull the thread to gather the circle, and tie a knot. Attach the berries to the quilt.

Embroider the Following:				
Location	**Color of Floss**	**Number of Strands**	**Stitch**	**Item to Embroider**
Center square	Black	4	Backstitch	Words
Center square	Black	1	Backstitch	Cord on top of bells
Center square	Black	3	Backstitch	Cord from ribbon to jingle bells, lines in jingle bells
Center square	Black	3	French knot	Holes in jingle bells

Finishing

1. Layer the quilt top with batting and backing; baste. Quilt as desired.
2. Bind the edges of the quilt.
3. Add a sleeve, if desired.

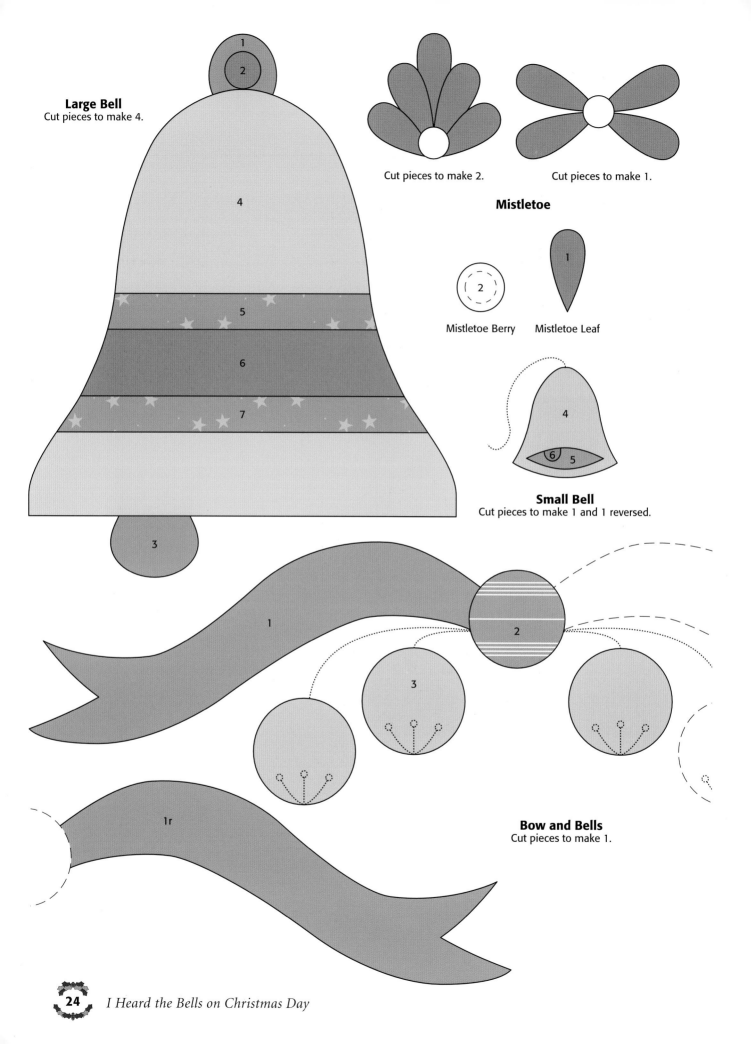

Large Bell
Cut pieces to make 4.

Cut pieces to make 2.

Cut pieces to make 1.

Mistletoe

Mistletoe Berry   Mistletoe Leaf

Small Bell
Cut pieces to make 1 and 1 reversed.

Bow and Bells
Cut pieces to make 1.

I Heard the Bells on Christmas Day

I HEARD THE BELLS ON CHRISTMAS DAY

Merry, Merry, Merry Christmas

Finished Quilt Size: 37½" x 37½"

MERRY, MERRY, MERRY CHRISTMAS *by Eileen Westfall, 1999, Walnut Creek, California. Hand quilted by Katherine Bilton. I love Christmas wreaths in all shapes, forms, and sizes. They have always been a part of my decorating style. Three of the wreaths in this piece have the word* Merry *and the last wreath has the word* Christmas, *wishing one and all a merry, merry, merry Christmas. This is a good quilt to hang in an entryway.*

MATERIALS

42"-wide fabric

¼ yd. red print #1 for striped units
⅛ yd. red print #2 for striped units
½ yd. green-and-red print for sashing
¾ yd. cream solid for background
½ yd. dark red print for inner border
¼ yd. red-and-white stripe for middle border
¼ yd. green-and-cream print for outer border
⅜ yd. for binding
Scraps of solids and prints in the following colors for appliqué: gold, light green, dark green, and red
1 skein of embroidery floss in each of the following colors: gold, dark green, and black
42" x 42" piece of batting
1¼ yds. for backing

CUTTING

From red print #1, cut:
   18 rectangles, each 1½" x 3½" (C)

From red print #2, cut:
   9 rectangles, each 1½" x 3½" (C)

From the green-and-red print, cut:
   12 strips, each 3½" x 11½" (B)

From the cream solid, cut:
   4 blocks, each 11½" x 11½" (A)

From the dark red print, cut:
   2 strips, each 1½" x 31½" (D)
   2 strips, each 1½" x 33½" (E)

From the red-and-white stripe, cut:
   2 strips, each 1½" x 33½" (F)
   2 strips, each 1½" x 35½" (G)

From the green-and-cream print, cut:
   2 strips, each 1½" x 35½" (H)
   2 strips, each 1½" x 37½" (I)

From the fabric for the binding, cut:
   4 strips, each 2" x 42"

PATCHWORK

1. Join 2 red print #1 C rectangles and 1 red print #2 C rectangles to make a striped unit. Make 9 units.

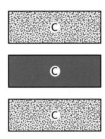

Make 9.

2. Join 2 green-and-red B strips and 3 striped units (orienting them as shown) to make each of 3 sashing rows. Join 2 cream A blocks, and 3 green-and-red B strips to make each of 2 rows. Join the rows of A squares and sashing rows.

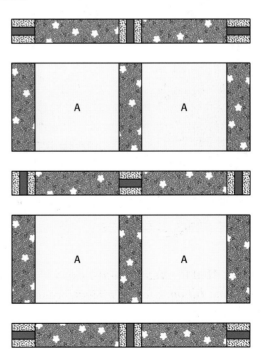

3. Add the dark red D strips to the sides first; then add the dark red E strips to the top and bottom edges.

4. Add the red-and-white F strips and G strips and green-and-cream H strips and I strips in the same manner as step 3.

APPLIQUÉ AND EMBROIDERY

Using the patterns on pages 29–30, prepare appliqué shapes following the directions for fusible appliqué on pages 9–10. Appliqué the pieces in numerical order.

EMBROIDER THE FOLLOWING:

Location	Color of Floss	Number of Strands	Stitch	Item to Embroider
Wreaths	Dark green	1	Backstitch	Vine on each side of leaves
Wreaths	Black or gold	4	Backstitch	Outline words
Wreaths	Dark green or gold	4	Backstitch	Outline ribbons and knot

FINISHING

1. Layer the quilt top with batting and backing; baste. Quilt as desired.
2. Bind the edges of the quilt.
3. Add a sleeve, if desired.

1
Prairie Point
Cut 72.

M
E
R
Y
C
H
IS
TA

Wreath

Place on fold.

Place on fold.

2
Cut 4.

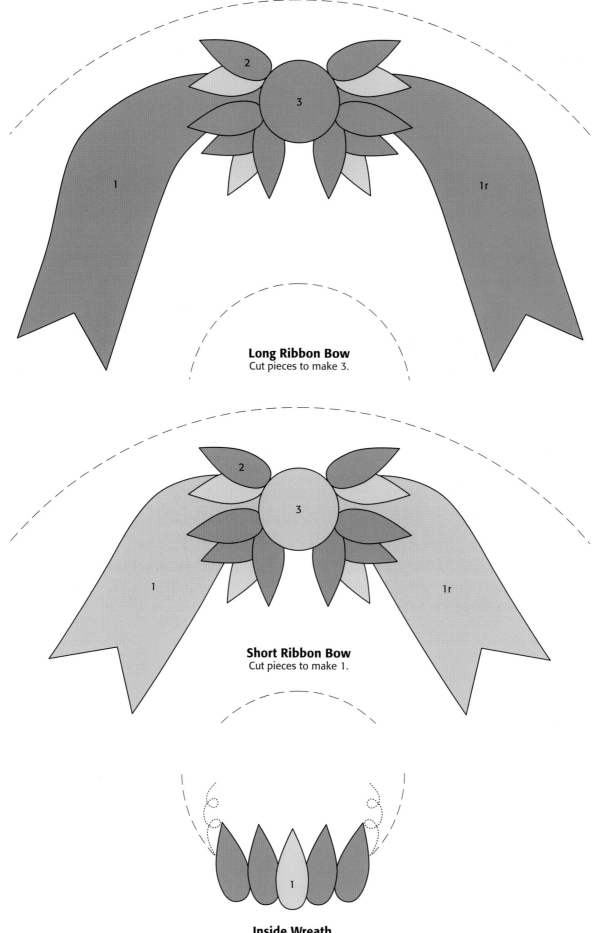

Long Ribbon Bow
Cut pieces to make 3.

Short Ribbon Bow
Cut pieces to make 1.

Inside Wreath
Cut pieces to make 4.

Mr. and Mrs. Bear's Christmas Brunch

Finished Quilt Size: 21½" x 37½"

***MR. AND MRS. BEAR'S CHRISTMAS BRUNCH** by Eileen Westfall, 1999, Walnut Creek, California. Hand quilted by Anna Stoltzfus. Everyone loves teddy bears and I am no exception. After I dressed the bears in their Christmas finery, I wondered what a bear's Christmas brunch would include. The answer came to me that bears love four things in their diet: berries, fish, honey, and porridge.*

MATERIALS

42"-wide fabric

⅛ yd. green check for four-patch units
⅜ yd. red-and-cream print for four-patch units
    and outer border
¼ yd. light purple print for background
¼ yd. light green solid for background
¼ yd. light pink print for background
¼ yd. medium purple print for sashing
⅜ yd. large-scale print for inner border
⅜ yd. for binding
Scraps in solids and prints in the following col-
    ors for appliqué: light brown, medium
    brown, light pink, dark pink, gray, and red
1 skein of embroidery floss in each of the follow-
    ing colors: red, brown, yellow, black, green,
    purple, pink, and bright pink
26" x 42" piece of batting
⅞ yd. for backing

CUTTING

From the green check, cut:
    16 squares, each 1½" x 1½" (E)

From the red-and-cream print, cut:
    16 squares, each 1½" x 1½" (E)
    2 strips, each 2½" x 17½" (H)
    2 strips, each 2½" x 37½" (I)

From the light purple print, cut:
    2 rectangles, each 4" x 5" (B)

From the light green solid, cut:
    1 rectangle, 7½" x 9½" (A)
    2 rectangles, each 4" x 5" (B)

From the light pink print, cut:
    1 rectangle, 7½" x 9½" (A)

From the medium purple print, cut:
    4 strips, each 2½" x 9½" (C)
    6 strips, each 2½" x 7½" (D)

From the large-scale print, cut:
    2 strips, each 2½" x 13½" (F)
    2 strips, each 2½" x 33½" (G)

From the fabric for the binding, cut:
    4 strips, each 2" x 42"

PATCHWORK

1. Join 2 green E squares and 2 red-and-cream E
   squares to make a four-patch unit. Make 8
   units.

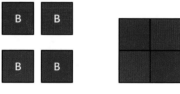

Make 8.

2. Join 2 light purple B rectangles and 2 light
   green B rectangles to make the center rectangle. Join the center rectangle, 1 light pink
   and 1 light green A rectangle, and 4 medium
   purple C strips to make the center row. Join 4
   four-patch units from step 1 and 3 medium
   purple D strips to make each of 2 rows. Add
   these to the top and bottom edges of the center row.

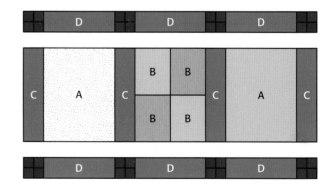

3. Add the large-scale print F strips to the sides first; then add the G strips to the top and bottom edges. Repeat with the red-and-cream strips, adding H first and then I.

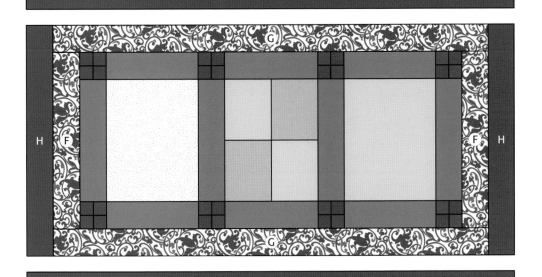

APPLIQUÉ AND EMBROIDERY

Using the patterns on pages 35–37, prepare appliqué shapes following the directions for fusible appliqué on pages 9–10. Appliqué the pieces in numerical order. Appliqué the ribbon on the Berries block after embroidering the branches, berries, and leaves.

EMBROIDER THE FOLLOWING:				
Location	**Color of Floss**	**Number of Strands**	**Stitch**	**Item to Embroider**
Bears	Black	1	Backstitch	Mouth, eyebrows, eyelashes
Bears	Black	1	Satin stitch	Eyes
Mrs. Bear	Pink	1	Satin stitch	Cheeks and tongue
Mrs. Bear	Bright pink	1	Satin stitch	Nose
Mr. Bear	Pink	1	Satin stitch	Tongue
Mr. Bear	Brown	1	Satin stitch	Nose
Mr. Bear	Red	1	Backstitch	Shoe strap
Honey pot	Black	1	Backstitch	Word
Honey pot	Black	1	Satin stitch	Bee body
Honey pot	Yellow	1	Satin stitch	Bee body
Porridge	Black	1	Backstitch	Word, steam rising from bowl

(Chart continued on next page)

Location	Color of Floss	Number of Strands	Stitch	Item to Embroider
Porridge	Red	1	Backstitch	Bowl details
Porridge	Red	1	Satin stitch	Bowl details
Porridge	Purple	1	Backstitch	Bowl details
Porridge	Purple	1	Satin stitch	Bowl details
Berries	Black	1	Backstitch	Word
Berries	Brown	1	Backstitch	Branches
Berries	Green	1	Satin stitch	Leaves
Berries	Red	1	Satin stitch	Berries
Fish	Black	1	Backstitch	Word, smiles, fins
Fish	Black	1	French knot	Eyes

FINISHING

1. Layer the quilt top with batting and backing; baste. Quilt as desired.
2. Bind the edges of the quilt.
3. Add a sleeve, if desired.

Mrs. Bear
Cut pieces to make 1.

Mr. Bear
Cut pieces to make 1.

Mr. and Mrs. Bear's Christmas Brunch

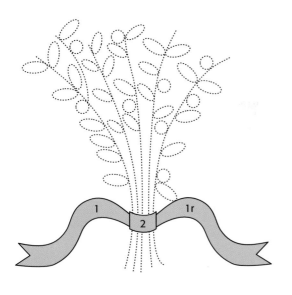

BERRIES

Cut pieces to make 1.

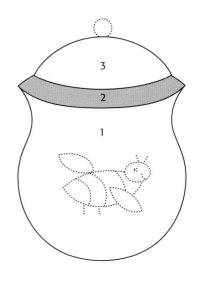

HONEY

Cut pieces to make 1.

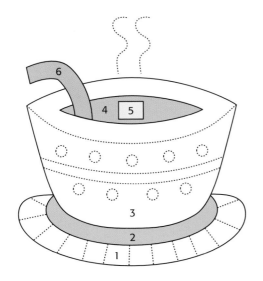

PORRIDGE

Cut pieces to make 1.

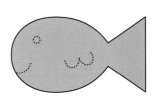

FISH

Cut 3.

Kitty's Christmas

Finished Quilt Size: 32½" x 32½"

KITTY'S CHRISTMAS by Eileen Westfall, 1999, Walnut Creek, California. Hand quilted by Anna Stoltzfus. I love cats as much as I love dogs. Though I don't currently have a cat, I have had many over the years. This quilt, which features a festively decorated kitty surrounded by stockings, balls of yarn, bags of catnip, and favorite toys, is made in memory of all my beloved feline friends—especially my Persian kitty, Anastasia.

MATERIALS

42"-wide fabric

⅛ yd. blue print for Puss in the Corner blocks

⅛ yd. red solid for Puss in the Corner blocks

⅛ yd. green print #1 for Puss in the Corner blocks

¼ light green solid #2 for Puss in the Corner blocks

⅛ yd. green print #2 for nine-patch units

⅛ yd. white-and-red print for nine-patch units

¼ yd. red-with-white-dots print for corner squares

¼ yd. white solid for background

¼ light green solid #1 for background

⅜ yd. gray print for inner and outer border

½ yd. white holiday print for middle border

⅜ yd. for binding

Scraps of solids and prints in the following colors for appliqué: light gray, medium gray, blue, red, green, pink, red-and-white striped, and gold

1 skein of embroidery floss in each of the following colors: black, green, and red

36" x 36" piece of batting

1 yd. for backing

CUTTING

From the blue print, cut:
20 squares, each 1½" x 1½" (C)

From the red solid, cut:
28 squares, each 1½" x 1½" (C)

From green print #1, cut:
40 squares, each 1½" x 1½" (C)

From the light green solid #2, cut:
16 squares, each 2½" x 2½" (B)

From green print #2, cut:
16 squares, each 1½" x 1½" (C)

From the white-and-red print, cut:
20 squares, each 1½" x 1½" (C)

From the red-with-white-dots print, cut:
8 rectangles, each 1½" x 3½" (F)
8 rectangles, each 1½" x 5½" (G)

From the white solid, cut:
4 squares, each 6½" x 6½" (A)

From the light green solid #1, cut:
1 square, 6½" x 6½" (A)

From the gray print, cut:
4 strips, each 1½" x 18½" (D)
4 strips, each 1½" x 30½" (H)

From the white holiday print, cut:
4 strips, each 5½" x 20½" (E)

From the fabric for the binding, cut:
4 strips, each 2" x 42"

PATCHWORK

1. Join 1 blue C square, 1 red C square, and 2 green print #1 C squares to make a four-patch unit. Make 20 units.

Make 20.

2. Join 5 four-patch units and 4 light green solid #2 B squares to make a Puss in the Corner block. Make 4 blocks.

Make 4.

3. Join 4 green print #2 C squares and 5 white-and-red C squares to make a nine-patch unit. Make 4 units.

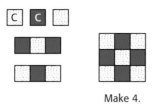

Make 4.

4. Join 1 nine-patch unit, 2 red-with-white-dots F rectangles, and 2 red-with-white-dots G rectangles to make a corner square. Make 4 squares.

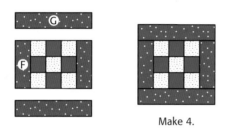

Make 4.

5. Join 4 white A squares, 1 light green solid #1 A square, and 4 Puss in the Corner blocks to complete the center section.

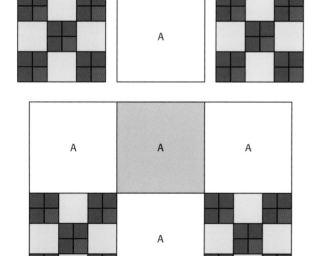

6. Add 2 gray D strips to the sides of the center section. Add a red C square to each of the remaining gray D strips and attach these strips to the top and bottom edges.

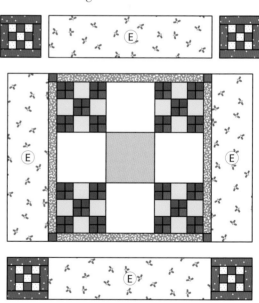

7. Join 2 white holiday print E strips to the sides. Add a corner square to each end of the remaining E strips and attach these to the top and bottom edges.

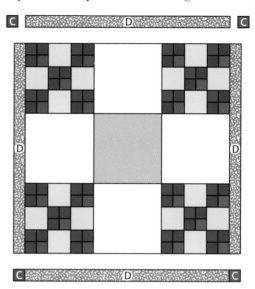

8. Join 2 gray H strips to the sides. Add a red C square to each of the remaining H strips and attach these to the top and bottom edges.

APPLIQUÉ AND EMBROIDERY

Using the patterns on pages 42–43, prepare appliqué shapes following the directions for fusible appliqué on pages 9–10. Appliqué the pieces in numerical order.

Location	Color of Floss	Number of Strands	Stitch	Item to Embroider
EMBROIDER THE FOLLOWING:				
Kitty head	Black	1	Backstitch	Eyelashes, eyebrows, mouth, whiskers, lines on bells, outline of eyes
Kitty head	Black	1	French knot	Dots on mouth, holes on bell
Stocking	Red	2	Backstitch	Word, loop on stocking
Stocking	Green	2	Backstitch	Word, loop on stocking
Fish	Black	1	Backstitch	Mouth, outer circle of eye on the fish
Fish	Green	1	Satin stitch	Pupil
Fish	Black	1	French knot	Nose
Catnip bag	Black	1	Backstitch	Word, drawstring, outline of bag lining

Make 1.

Make 2.

Make 2.

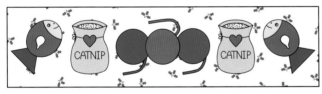

Make 4.

FINISHING

1. Layer the quilt top with batting and backing; baste. Quilt as desired.
2. Bind the edges of the quilt.
3. Add a sleeve, if desired.

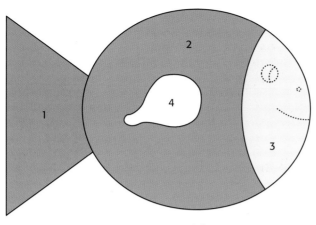

Fish
Cut pieces to make 4 and 4 reversed.

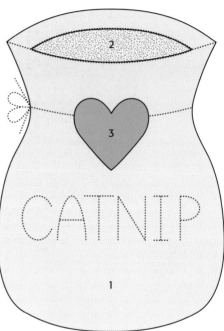

Catnip Bag
Cut pieces to make 8.

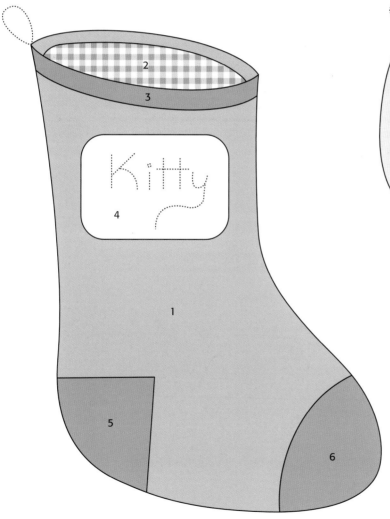

Stocking
Cut pieces to make 4.

Kitty
Cut pieces to make 1.

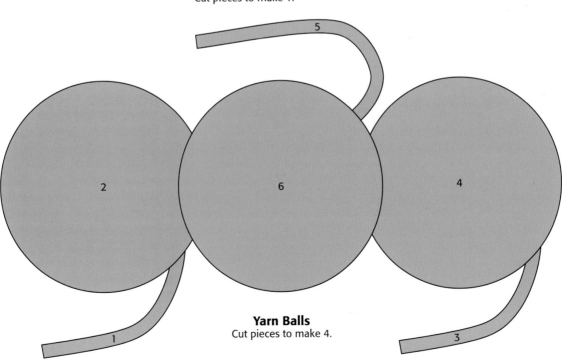

Yarn Balls
Cut pieces to make 4.

Birds of a Feather Celebrate Together

Finished Quilt Size: 33½" x 35½"

BIRDS OF A FEATHER CELEBRATE TOGETHER by Eileen Westfall, 1999, Walnut Creek, California. Hand quilted by Anna Stolzfus. Bright red cardinals are shown celebrating their favorite holiday. Even their birdhouse is decorated with lights and a welcoming sign. What a perfect quilt for a bird watcher.

MATERIALS

42"-wide fabric

½ yd. red print for corner squares and first, third, and fifth borders

½ yd. light blue solid for center square

⅜ yd. green-and-white print for second and sixth borders

⅛ yd. black print for corner squares

⅛ yd. black-and-tan check for corner squares

⅛ yd. white-and-red print for corner squares

⅜ yd. white solid for fourth border

⅜ yd. multicolored print for seventh border

⅜ yd. for binding

Scraps of solids and prints in the following colors for appliqué: red, black, light brown, medium brown, light green, medium green, blue, yellow, and gray,

1 skein of embroidery floss in the following colors: black and red

38" x 40" piece of batting

1⅛ yds. for backing

CUTTING

From the red print, cut:
2 strips, each 1½" x 11½"(B)
2 strips, each 1½" x 15½" (C)
2 strips, each 1½" x 15½" (G)
2 strips, each 1½" x 17½" (H)
2 strips, each 1½" x 25½" (L)
2 strips, each 1½" x 27½" (M)
4 squares, each 2⅞" x 2⅞". Cut once diagonally to make 8 triangles (I).

From the light blue solid, cut:
1 rectangle, 11½" x 13½" (A)

From the green-and-white print, cut:
2 strips, each 1½" x 13½" (E)
2 strips, each 1½" x 15½" (F)
2 strips, each 1½" x 27½" (N)
2 strips, each 1½" x 29½" (O)

From the black print, cut:
32 squares, each 1½" x 1½" (D)

From the black-and-tan check, cut:
4 squares, each 2⅞" x 2⅞". Cut once diagonally to make 8 triangles (I).

From the white-and-red print, cut:
16 squares, each 1½" x 1½" (D)

From the white solid, cut:
2 rectangles, each 4½" x 17½" (J)
2 rectangles, each 4½" x 19½" (K)

From the multicolored print, cut:
2 strips, each 2½" x 29½" (P)
2 strips, each 2½" x 35½" (Q)

From the fabric for the binding, cut:
4 strips, each 2" x 42"

PATCHWORK

1. Join 2 red B strips to opposite sides of the light blue A rectangle. Add 2 red C strips to the top and bottom edges.

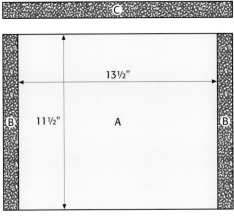

2. Join 2 green-and-white E strips to the sides of the center section. Add a black D square to each end of the green-and-white F strips and attach these to the top and bottom edges.

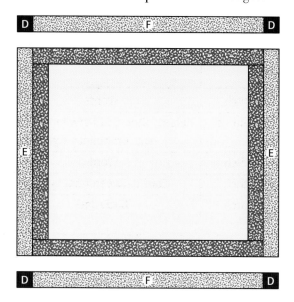

3. Join 2 red G strips to opposite sides. Add a black D square to each end of the red H strips and attach these to the top and bottom edges.

4. Join 1 black-and-tan I triangle and 1 red I triangle to make a triangle unit. Make 8. Join 2 white-and-red D squares and 2 black D squares to make a four-patch unit. Make 8. Join the triangle units and four-patch units to make a corner square. Make 4 squares.

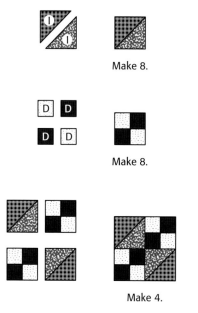

Make 8.

Make 8.

Make 4.

5. Join 2 white J rectangles to the sides. Add a corner square to each end of the white K rectangles and attach these to the top and bottom edges.

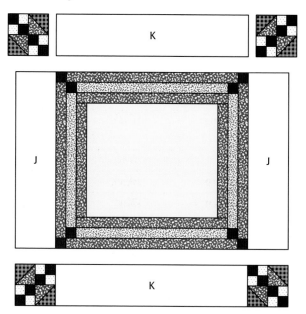

6. Add the red L strips to the sides first. Add a black D square to each end of the red M strips and attach these to the top and bottom edges. Repeat with the green-and-white N strips and O strips and 4 black D squares.

7. Add the multicolored P strips to the sides first; then add the multicolored Q strips to the top and bottom edges.

APPLIQUÉ AND EMBROIDERY

Using the patterns on pages 48–50, prepare appliqué shapes following the directions for fusible appliqué on pages 9–10. Appliqué the pieces in numerical order.

EMBROIDER THE FOLLOWING:				
Location	**Color of Floss**	**Number of Strands**	**Stitch**	**Item to Embroider**
Center square	Black	4	Backstitch	Words
Center square	Black	3	French knots	Before, after, and between words; nails on holiday sign
Birdhouse	Red	1	Backstitch	Words
Center square	Black	2	Backstitch	Cord between mini lights
Center square and border	Black	1	Backstitch	Bird's feet
Border	Black	1	Backstitch	Top loop on ornaments

Make 1.

Make 4.

FINISHING

1. Layer the quilt top with batting and backing; baste. Quilt as desired.
2. Bind the edges of the quilt.
3. Add a sleeve, if desired.

Bird on Branch
Cut all pieces to make 1 and 1 reversed.
Cut pieces 11–15 to make 8 additional cardinals for the borders.

Border Ornament
Cut pieces to make 8.

Border Package
Cut pieces to make 12.

Birdhouse
Cut pieces to make 1.

HAPPY HOLIDAYS

BIRDS OF A FEATHER

CELEBRATE TOGETHER

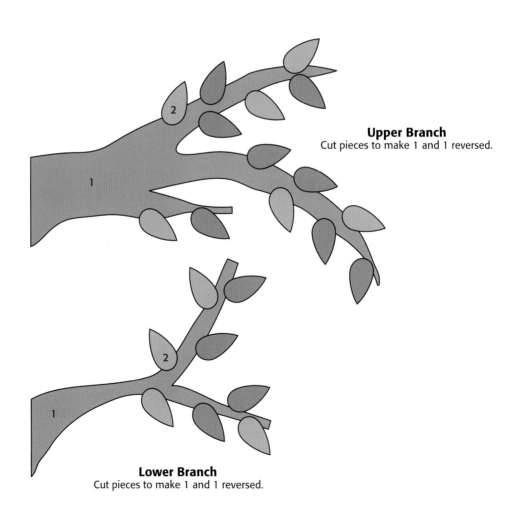

Upper Branch
Cut pieces to make 1 and 1 reversed.

Lower Branch
Cut pieces to make 1 and 1 reversed.

Dog Days of Christmas

Finished Quilt Size: 35½" x 41½"

***DOG DAYS OF CHRISTMAS** by Eileen Westfall, 1999, Walnut Creek, California. Hand quilted by Anna Stoltzfus. I am an animal lover and wanted to make a holiday quilt for our cocker spaniel, Josie. He was my inspiration for much of this quilt. Josie is forever chewing on a bone of rawhide, so the quilt has lots of bones in it—twenty to be exact! The dogs are sporting holly decorations in their hair and red ribbons around their necks, something Josie would never allow! I know that Josie would love his own fire hydrant, so for good measure, I put in two.*

MATERIALS

42"-wide fabric

¼ yd. red print for pieced blocks and corner squares

⅛ yd. blue print for pieced blocks

¼ yd. dark green print for pieced blocks and corner squares

⅛ yd. yellow print for pieced blocks and corner squares

1 yd. white solid for pieced blocks and middle border

⅜ yd. light blue solid for background

¾ yd. striped fabric for sashing, and inner and outer borders

⅜ yd. for binding

¼ yd. gold-and-brown print for dog appliqué

Scraps of solids and prints in the following colors for appliqué: light green, light red, light brown, medium brown, dark brown, and black

1 skein embroidery floss in the following colors: dark brown, medium brown, black, and white

40" x 46" piece of batting

1¼ yds. for backing

CUTTING

From the red print, cut:

4 squares, each 2⅞" x 2⅞". Cut once diagonally to make 8 triangles (B).

8 squares, each 2½" x 2½" (J)

From the blue print, cut:

4 squares, each 2⅞" x 2⅞". Cut once diagonally to make 8 triangles (B)

From the dark green print, cut:

8 squares, each 2⅞" x 2⅞". Cut once diagonally to make 16 triangles (B).

From the yellow print, cut:

8 squares, each 2⅞" x 2⅞". Cut once diagonally to make 16 triangles (B).

From the white solid, cut:

8 rectangles, each 2½" x 4½" (A)

2 strips, each 4½" x 24½" (I)

2 strips, each 4½" x 30½" (H)

From the light blue solid, cut:

6 rectangles, each 5½" x 8½" (C)

1 square, 8½" x 8½" (D)

From the striped fabric, cut:

6 strips, each 2" x 8½" (E)

4 strips, each 2" x 21½" (F)

2 strips, each 2" x 30½" (G)

2 strips, each 2" x 38½" (K)

2 strips, each 2" x 35½" (L)

From the fabric for the binding, cut:

4 strips, each 2" x 42"

PATCHWORK

1. Join a red B triangle and a blue B triangle to make a red/blue unit. Make 8 units. Repeat with a dark green B triangle and a yellow B triangle to make a dark green/yellow unit. Make 16 units.

Make 8.

Make 16.

2. Join 4 red/blue units, 4 dark green/yellow units, and 4 white A rectangles to make a block. Make 2 blocks.

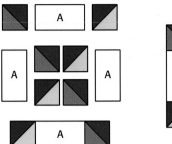
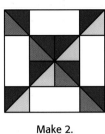

Make 2.

3. Join 2 light blue C rectangles, 2 striped fabric E pieces, and a block made in step 2 to make each of the top and bottom rows. Join 2 light blue C rectangles, 2 striped fabric E pieces, and 1 light blue D square to make the middle row. Join the top, middle, and bottom rows, adding the striped fabric F pieces between the rows and to the top and bottom edges. Add 2 striped fabric G pieces to the sides.

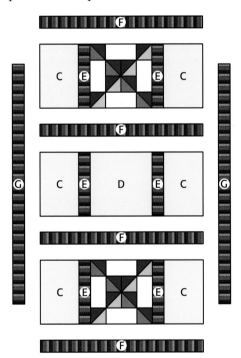

4. Join 2 dark green/yellow units and 2 red J squares to make a corner square. Make 4 squares.

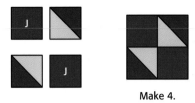

Make 4.

5. Join 2 white H strips to the sides of the quilt. Add a corner square to each end of the white I pieces and attach these to the top and bottom edges of the quilt.

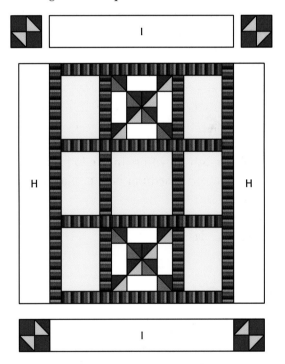

6. Add the striped fabric K strips to the sides first; then add the striped fabric L strips to the top and bottom edges.

Using the patterns on pages 55–56, prepare appliqué shapes following the directions for fusible appliqué on pages 9–10. Appliqué the pieces in numerical order.

Location	Color of Floss	Number of Strands	Stitch	Item to Embroider
EMBROIDER THE FOLLOWING:				
Dogs	Medium brown	2	Backstitch	Eyebrows, eyelashes, outline eyes
Dogs	White	2	Satin stitch	Eye highlight
Dogs	Black	2	Backstitch	Whiskers, lines on paws
Dogs	Dark brown	4	Backstitch	Outline of body and head
Fire hydrants	Black	2	Backstitch	Lines

Make 1.   Make 4.   Make 2.

Make 2.

Make 2.

Finishing

1. Layer the quilt top with batting and backing; baste. Quilt as desired.
2. Bind the edges of the quilt.
3. Add a sleeve, if desired.

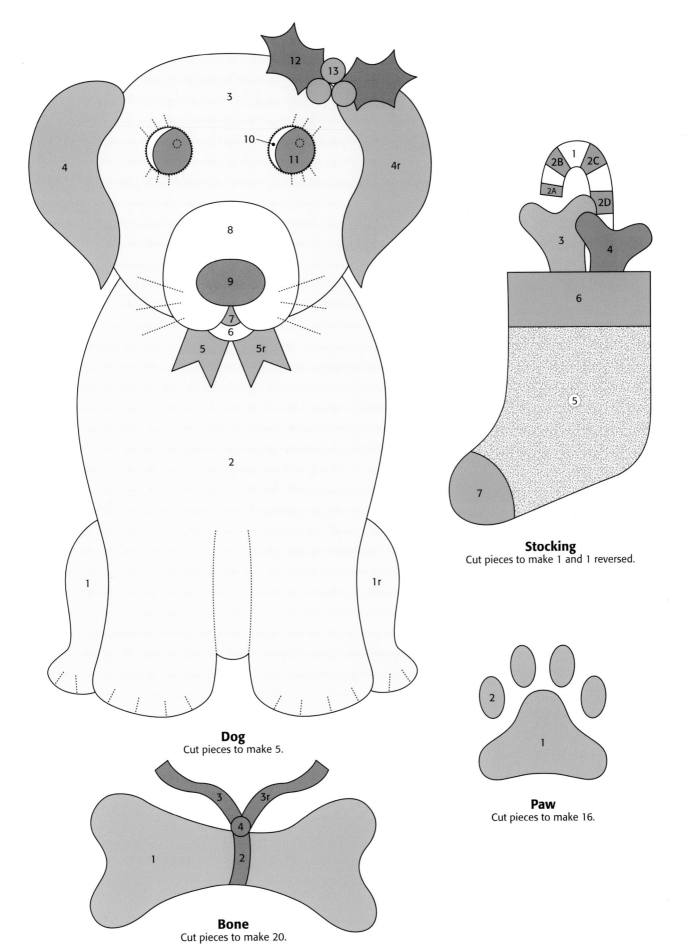

Dog
Cut pieces to make 5.

Stocking
Cut pieces to make 1 and 1 reversed.

Paw
Cut pieces to make 16.

Bone
Cut pieces to make 20.

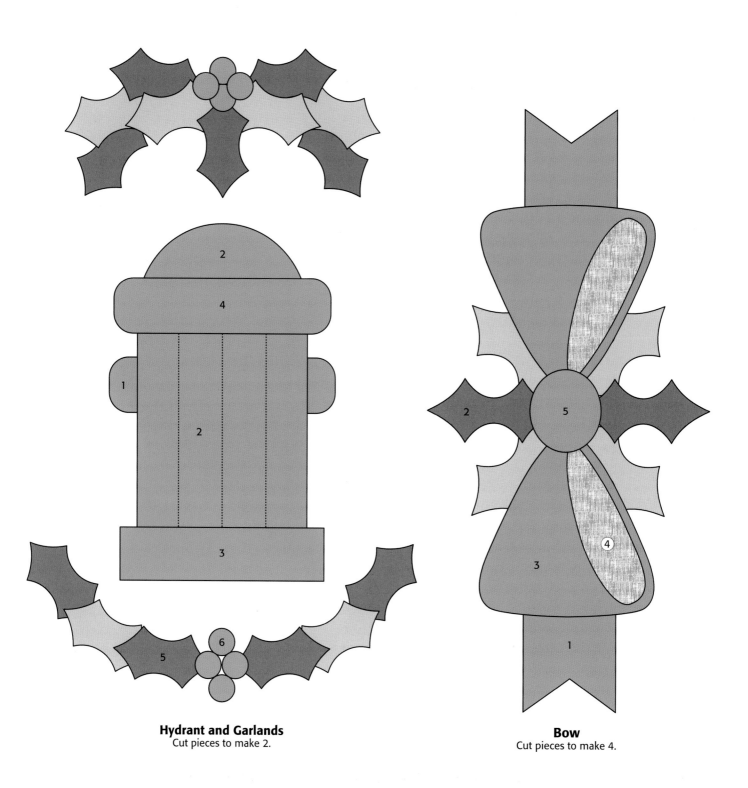

Hydrant and Garlands
Cut pieces to make 2.

Bow
Cut pieces to make 4.

 # 'Tis Better to Give Than Receive

Finished Quilt Size: 31½" x 31½"

'TIS BETTER TO GIVE THAN RECEIVE *by Eileen Westfall, 1999, Walnut Creek, California. Hand quilted by Diana Near. This verse from the Bible reminds us of the joy of giving and the spirit of Christmas. Gifts with bows and gift tags are the focal point of the center block and are ready to be given away. The corner squares with the heart in the open hand represent love, reminding us again of the true meaning of the season.*

MATERIALS

42"-wide fabric

2" x 4" piece of light green-and-white print for
  corner squares
2" x 4" piece of dark green solid for corner
  squares
½ yd. white solid for center square, second top
  and bottom borders, and corner squares
⅛ yd. light brown solid for center square
¼ yd. red print #1 for first border
4" x 6" piece of red-and-white check for second
  border
⅜ yd. multicolored print for third border
½ yd. red print #2 for fourth border
⅜ yd. for binding
Scraps in solids and prints in the following colors for appliqué: red, green, blue, and yellow
4½" x 6" piece of green print for left package
4½" x 6" piece of red print #3 for right package
5½" x 5" piece of blue print for center package
1 skein of navy blue embroidery floss
36" x 36" piece of batting
1 yd. for backing

CUTTING

From the light green-and-white print, cut:
  2 squares, each 1⅞" x 1⅞". Cut once diago-
    nally to make 4 triangles (C).

From the dark green solid, cut:
  2 squares, each 1⅞" x 1⅞". Cut once diago-
    nally to make 4 triangles (C).

From the white solid, cut:
  1 rectangle, 8½" x 15½" (A)
  2 strips, each 2½" x 15½" (F)
  4 squares, each 4½" x 4½" (I)

From the light brown solid, cut:
  1 strip, 3½" x 15½" (B)

From red print #1, cut:
  2 strips, each 1½" x 11½" (D)
  2 strips, each 1½" x 15½" (E)

From the red-and-white check, cut:
  4 rectangles, each 1½" x 2½" (G)

From the multicolored print, cut:
  4 strips, each 4½" x 17½" (H)

From red print #2, cut:
  2 strips, each 3½" x 25½" (J)
  2 strips, each 3½" x 31½" (K)

From the fabric for the binding, cut:
  4 strips, each 2" x 42"

PATCHWORK

1. Join 1 light green-and-white C triangle and 1
   dark green C triangle to make a triangle unit.

Make 4.

2. Join the white A rectangle and the light
   brown B strip. Add 1 red print #1 D strip to
   each side. Add a triangle unit from step 1 to
   each end of the red print #1 E strips and
   attach these to the top and bottom edges.

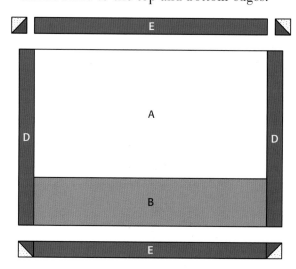

3. Join a red-and-white G rectangle to each end of the white F strips. Attach these to the top and bottom of the center section. Join 2 multi-colored H strips to the sides. Add a white I square to each end of the remaining H strips, and attach these to the top and bottom edges.

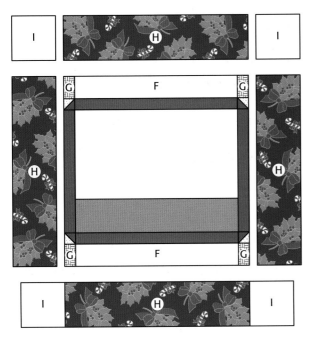

4. Add the red print #2 J strips to the sides first; then add the red print #2 K strips to the top and bottom edges.

APPLIQUÉ AND EMBROIDERY

Using the patterns on pages 60–61, prepare appliqué shapes following the directions for fusible appliqué on pages 9–10. Appliqué the pieces in numerical order. Cut pieces for packages as follows:

4" x 5⅜" from green print
3¾" x 5¼" from red print #3
5" x 4⅜" from blue print

EMBROIDER THE FOLLOWING:				
Location	Color of Floss	Number of Strands	Stitch	Item to Embroider
D strips	Navy blue	4	Backstitch	Words
Gift tags	Navy blue	1	Backstitch	Label

Make 1.

Make 4.

FINISHING

1. Layer the quilt top with batting and backing; baste. Quilt as desired.
2. Bind the edges of the quilt.
3. Add a sleeve, if desired.

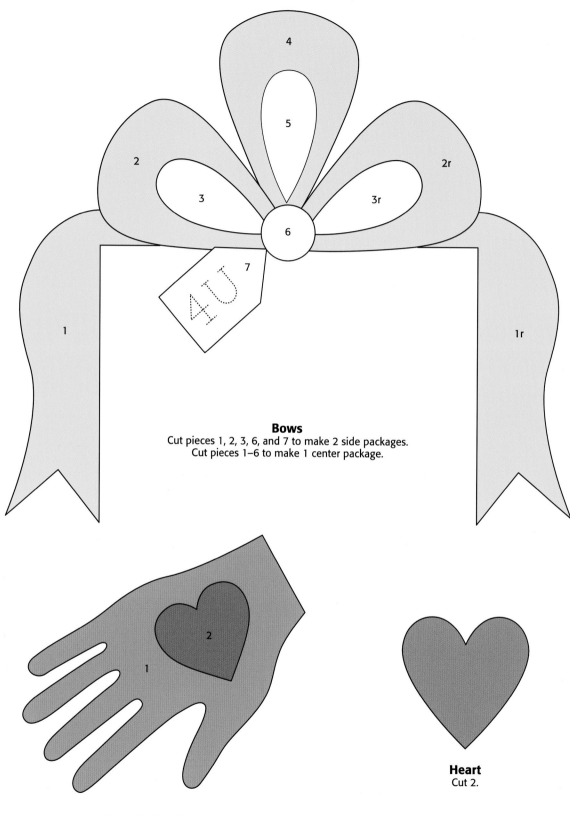

Bows
Cut pieces 1, 2, 3, 6, and 7 to make 2 side packages.
Cut pieces 1–6 to make 1 center package.

Heart in Hand
Cut pieces to make 4.

Heart
Cut 2.

Dutch Treat

Finished Quilt Size: 35½" x 35½"

DUTCH TREAT *by Eileen Westfall, 1999, Walnut Creek, California. Hand quilted by Anna Stoltzfus. When I took my first quilting class in 1977, my teacher, Ruth Briggs, gave us lots of classic patchwork and quilting patterns. One of them was of a Dutch wooden shoe filled with tulips. When I was thinking of quilt designs for this book, I remembered that pattern. I also remembered the tradition in Holland of having children leave wooden shoes out at night in early December for St. Nicholas to fill with goodies. The patchwork block used in this piece is the classic Dutchman's Puzzle. Several of the fabrics used in this quilt were purchased at the European Quilt Market in Innsbruck in 1998.*

MATERIALS

42"-wide fabric

⅛ yd. dark green solid for Dutchman's Puzzle blocks

¾ yd. white solid for background

⅛ yd. multicolored print for Dutchman's Puzzle blocks and side blocks

⅛ yd. pink-and-white print for side blocks

⅝ yd. poinsettia print for Pinwheel blocks and outer border

½ yd. light green print for sashing and inner border

⅛ yd. light and dark purple print for middle border

⅜ yd. for binding

Scraps of solids and prints in the following colors for appliqué: light pink, bright pink, light brown, medium brown, dark brown, cranberry, and medium green

1 skein of embroidery floss in each of the following colors: dark green and light brown

40" x 40" piece of batting

1⅛ yds. for backing

CUTTING

From the dark green solid, cut:

8 squares, each 2⅞" x 2⅞". Cut once diagonally to make 16 triangles (A).

From the white solid, cut:

32 squares, each 2⅞" x 2⅞". Cut once diagonally to make 64 triangles (A).

2 squares, each 8½" x 8½" (B)

8 squares, each 4½" x 4½" (H)

From the multicolored print, cut:

12 squares, each 2⅞" x 2⅞". Cut once diagonally to make 24 triangles (A).

From the pink-and-white print, cut:

4 squares, each 2⅞" x 2⅞". Cut once diagonally to make 8 triangles (A).

From the poinsettia print, cut:

8 squares, each 2⅞" x 2⅞". Cut once diagonally to make 16 triangles (A).

2 strips, each 3½" x 29½" (K)

2 strips, each 3½" x 35½" (L)

From the light green print, cut:

2 strips, each 1½" x 8½" (C)

3 strips, each 1½" x 17½" (D)

2 strips, each 1½" x 19½" (E)

16 rectangles, each 1½" x 4½" (F)

2 strips, each 1½" x 27½" (I)

2 strips, each 1½" x 29½" (J)

From the light and dark purple print, cut:

8 rectangles, each 2" x 4½" (G)

From the fabric for the binding, cut:

4 strips, each 2" x 42"

PATCHWORK

1. Join a dark green A triangle and a white A triangle to make Unit 1. Make 16. Join a multicolored A triangle and a white A triangle to make Unit 2. Make 24. Join a pink-and-white A triangle and a white A triangle to make Unit 3. Make 8. Join a poinsettia A triangle and a white A triangle to make Unit 4. Make 16.

Unit 1
Make 16.

Unit 2
Make 24.

Unit 3
Make 8.

Unit 4
Make 16.

2. Join 8 of Unit 1 and 8 of Unit 2 to make a Dutchman's Puzzle block. Make 2 blocks.

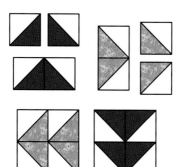

Make 2.

3. Join 2 of Unit 3 and 2 of Unit 4 to make a side block. Make 4 blocks.

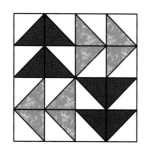

Side block
Make 4.

4. Join 4 of Unit 4 to make a Pinwheel block for the corner square. Make 4 blocks.

Corner square
Make 4.

5. Join 2 Dutchman's Puzzle blocks, 2 white B squares, 2 light green C strips, and 1 light green D strip to make the center section. Join the remaining light green D strips to the sides; then add the light green E strips to the top and bottom edges.

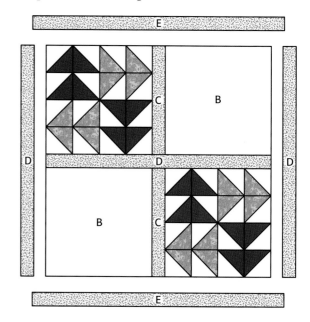

6. Join 1 side block, 4 light green F pieces, 2 light and dark purple G pieces, and 2 white H pieces to make each of the 4 pieced borders.

Make 4.

7. Join 2 pieced borders to the sides of the center section. Add a corner square to the remaining pieced borders and attach these to the top and bottom edges.

8. Add the light green I strips to the sides first; then add the light green J strips to the top and bottom edges. Repeat with the poinsettia K strips and L strips.

APPLIQUÉ AND EMBROIDERY

Using the patterns on page 66, prepare appliqué shapes following the directions for fusible appliqué on pages 9–10 Appliqué the pieces in numerical order.

EMBROIDER THE FOLLOWING:				
Location	Color of Floss	Number of Strands	Stitch	Item to Embroider
Shoes	Dark green	1	Backstitch	Sprig
Shoes	Light brown	2	Backstitch	Line between top and side

Make 1 and 1 reversed.

Make 8.

FINISHING

1. Layer the quilt top with batting and backing; baste. Quilt as desired.
2. Bind the edges of the quilt.
3. Add a sleeve, if desired.

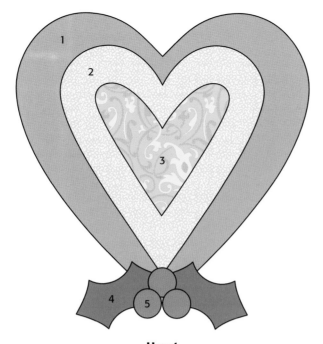

Heart
Cut pieces to make 8.

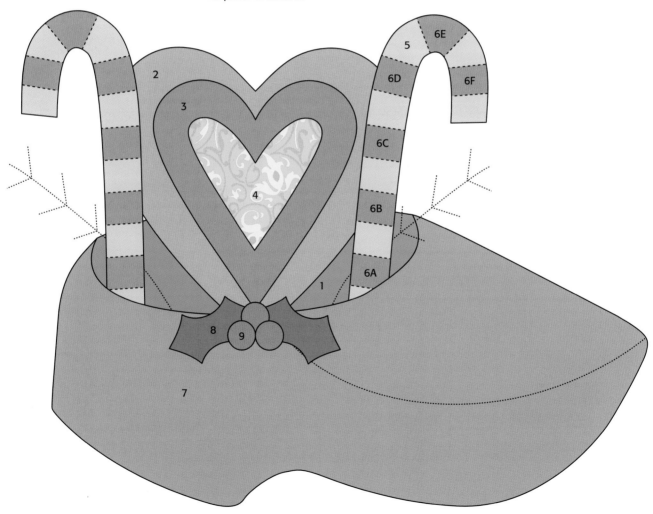

Wooden Shoe
Cut pieces to make 1 and 1 reversed.

Candles for Christmas

Finished Size: 28½" x 32½"

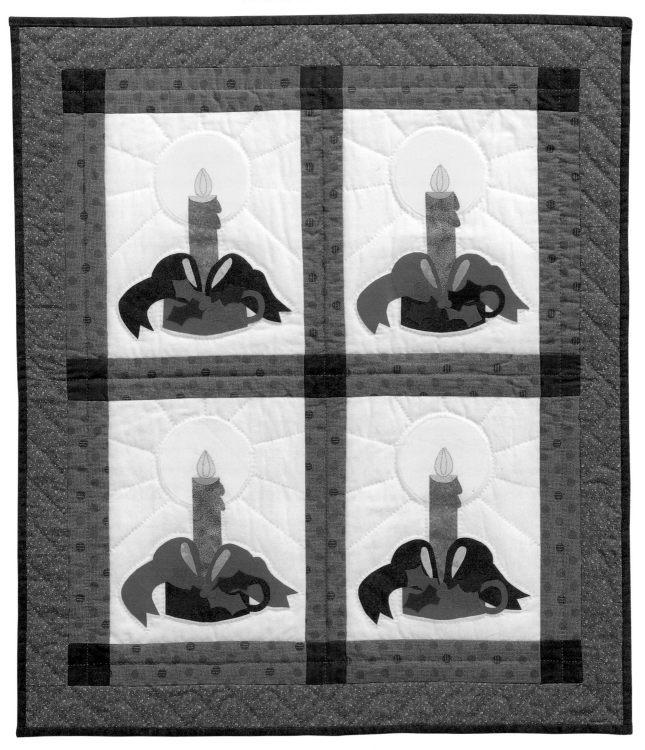

CANDLES FOR CHRISTMAS by Eileen Westfall, 1999, Walnut Creek, California. Hand quilted by Kim Chan. I read that in Ireland (land of my ancestors) the people always put a candle in the window at Christmas so that Father Christmas can find his way to their house to deliver their gifts. That tradition is what I had in mind when I created this quilt.

MATERIALS

42"-wide fabric

½ yd. white solid for background
⅜ yd. green-and-red print for sashing
⅛ yd. dark blue print for sashing squares
⅛ yd. bright green print for sashing squares
⅜ yd. multicolored print for outer border
⅜ yd. for binding
Scraps of solids and prints in the following colors for appliqué: light blue, navy blue, light green, medium green, red, pink, pale yellow, and bright yellow
1 skein of dark yellow embroidery floss
33" x 37" piece of batting
1 yd. for backing

CUTTING

From the white solid, cut:
4 rectangles, each 9½" x 11½" (A)

From the green-and-red print, cut:
6 strips, each 2½" x 11½" (B)
6 strips, each 2½" x 9½" (C)

From the dark blue print, cut:
5 squares, each 2½" x 2½" (D)

From the bright green print, cut:
4 squares, each 2½" x 2½" (D)

From the multicolored print, cut:
4 strips, each 2½" x 28½" (E)

From the fabric for the binding, cut:
4 strips, each 2" x 42"

PATCHWORK

1. Join 2 white A rectangles and 3 green-and-red B strips to make each of 2 rows. Join 2 dark blue D squares, 1 bright green D square, and 2 green-and-red C strips to make each of the top and bottom sashing rows. Join 1 dark blue D square, 2 bright green D squares, and 2 green-and-red C strips to make the middle sashing row. Join the 2 rows of A rectangles and B strips with the sashing rows.

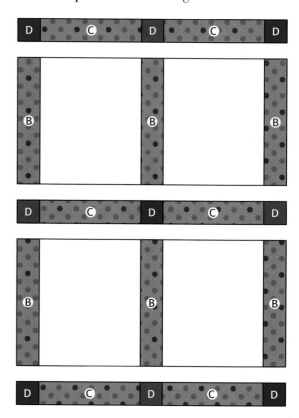

2. Add 2 of the multicolored E strips to the sides first; then add the remaining 2 E strips to the top and bottom edges.

APPLIQUÉ AND EMBROIDERY

Using the patterns on page 70, prepare appliqué shapes following the directions for fusible appliqué on pages 9–10. Appliqué the pieces in numerical order.

EMBROIDER THE FOLLOWING:				
Location	Color of Floss	Number of Strands	Stitch	Item to Embroider
Candle flame	Dark yellow	3	Backstitch	Inner flame lines, flame outline

Make 2.

Make 2.

FINISHING

1. Layer the quilt top with batting and backing; baste. Quilt as desired.
2. Bind the edges of the quilt.
3. Add a sleeve, if desired.

Placement for piece 8

Christmas Goodies

Finished Quilt Size: 16½" x 36½"

CHRISTMAS GOODIES *by Eileen Westfall, 1999, Walnut Creek, California. Hand quilted by Anna Stoltzfus. Everyone has special things they like to bake for the holiday season. For many years my son and I made a gingerbread house at the beginning of December. Making that house together was a wonderful tradition. In* A Christmas Carol, *the Cratchit family gobbles up a baked plum pudding. And love it or hate it, everyone has a fruitcake story to tell! All these holiday foods provided the inspiration for this quilt.*

MATERIALS

42"-wide fabric

⅛ yd. cranberry solid for sashing squares
⅛ yd. cranberry-and-cream check for sashing
  squares
¼ yd. dark cranberry-and-green print for sashing
⅜ yd. white-and-cream print for background
⅜ yd. medium green-and-cranberry print for
  border
¼ yd. for binding
Scraps of solids and prints in the following colors for appliqué: white, yellow, medium
  green, dark green, light brown, medium
  brown, and orange,
1 skein of embroidery floss in each of the following colors: medium brown and dark brown
20" x 40" piece of batting
⅝ yd. for backing

CUTTING

From the cranberry solid, cut:
  5 squares, each 3¼" x 3¼". Cut twice diago-
    nally to make 20 triangles (A).

From the cranberry-and-cream check, cut:
  5 squares, each 3¼" x 3¼". Cut twice diago-
    nally to make 20 triangles (A).

From the dark cranberry-and-green print, cut:
  4 rectangles, each 2½" x 3½" (B)
  8 rectangles, each 2½" x 8½" (D)

From the white-and-cream print, cut:
  3 squares, each 8½" x 8½" (C)

**From the medium green-and-cranberry print,
cut:**
  2 strips, each 2½" x 32½" (E)
  2 strips, each 2½" x 16½" (F)

From the fabric for the binding, cut:
  3 strips, each 2" x 42"

PATCHWORK

1. Join 2 cranberry solid A triangles and 2
   cranberry-and-cream A triangles to make a
   triangle unit. Make 10 units.

Make 10.

2. Join 2 triangle units and 1 dark cranberry-
   and-green D strip to make each of the top and
   bottom sashing rows. Join 3 triangle units
   and 2 dark cranberry-and-green B rectangles
   to make each of the 2 middle sashing rows.
   Join 1 white-and-cream C square and 2 dark
   cranberry-and-green D strips to make each of
   the 3 block rows. Join the rows of blocks and
   sashing rows.

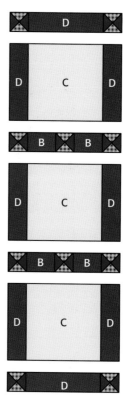

3. Add 2 medium green-and-cranberry E strips
   to the sides first; then add the 2 medium
   green-and-cranberry F strips to the top and
   bottom edges.

APPLIQUÉ AND EMBROIDERY

Using the patterns on pages 73–74, prepare appliqué shapes following the directions for fusible appliqué on pages 9–10. Appliqué the pieces in numerical order.

EMBROIDER THE FOLLOWING:				
Location	**Color of Floss**	**Number of Strands**	**Stitch**	**Item to Embroider**
Gingerbread house	Medium brown	1	Backstitch	Window lines
Fruitcake	Dark brown	1	Backstitch	Line between top and sides

Make 1.

Make 1.

Make 1.

FINISHING

1. Layer the quilt top with batting and backing; baste. Quilt as desired.
2. Bind the edges with bias strips.
3. Add a sleeve, if desired.

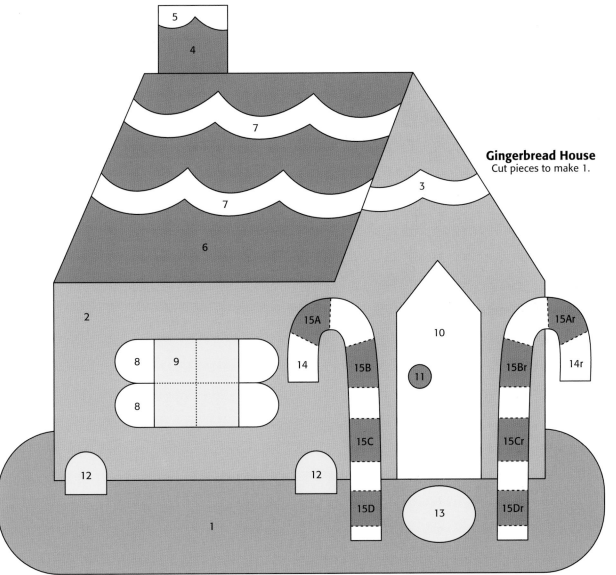

Gingerbread House
Cut pieces to make 1.

Plum Pudding
Cut pieces to make 1.

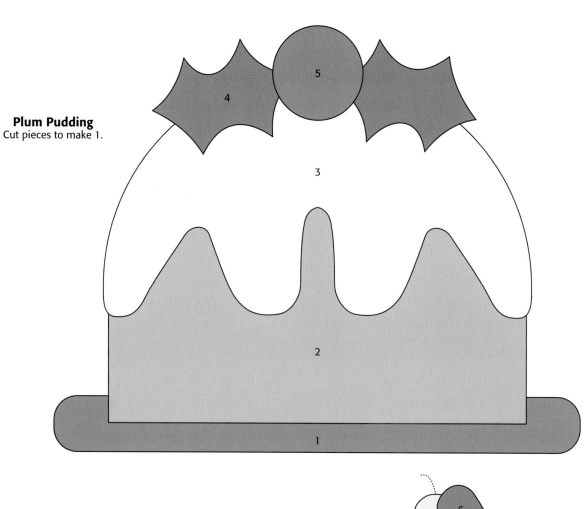

Fruitcake
Cut pieces to make 1.

Christmas Is Coming

Finished Quilt Size: 26½" x 38½"

CHRISTMAS IS COMING by Eileen Westfall, 1999, Walnut Creek, California. Hand quilted by Donna Remorini. About ten years ago I received a Christmas card featuring a fat goose and this famous English saying. When I found the card in my files, I decided it was time to make it into a quilt for this book.

MATERIALS

42"-wide fabric

⅜ yd. multicolored print for background
⅛ yd. red-and-gold check for background
⅛ yd. bright yellow print for first border
⅜ yd. white solid for second border
6" x 6" square of light gold print for corner
   squares
⅛ yd. yellow-and-green print for third border
6" x 6" piece red-and-white print for triangle
   units
3" x 6" piece of red-and-cream check for triangle
   units
6" x 6" piece dark green print for triangle units
3" x 6" piece of green-and-cream check for triangle units
¼ yd. cream-and-white print for hat background
½ yd. medium green print for fourth border
⅜ yd. for binding
Scraps of solids and prints in the following colors for appliqué: red, yellow, green, medium
   brown, black, gold, green-and-cream, black-
   and-tan, red-and-white, and gray
1 skein of black embroidery floss
30" x 42" piece of batting
⅞ yd. for backing

CUTTING

From the multicolored print, cut:
   1 rectangle, 9½" x 12½" (A)

From the red-and-gold check:, cut:
   1 rectangle. 3½" x 12½" (B)

From the bright yellow print, cut:
   2 strips, each 1½" x 12½" (C)
   2 strips, each 1½" x 14½" (D)

From the white solid, cut:
   4 strips, each 2½" x 14½" (E)
   12 squares, each 2⅞" x 2⅞". Cut once diago-
      nally to make 24 triangles (I).

From the light gold print, cut:
   4 squares, each 2½" x 2½" (F)

From the yellow-and-green print, cut:
   2 strips, each 1½" x 18½" (G)
   2 strips, each 1½" x 20½" (H)

From the red-and-white print, cut:
   4 squares, each 2⅞" x 2⅞". Cut once diago-
      nally to make 8 triangles (I).

From the red-and-cream check, cut:
   2 squares, each 2⅞" x 2⅞". Cut once diago-
      nally to make 4 triangles (I).

From the dark green print, cut:
   4 squares, each 2⅞" x 2⅞". Cut once diago-
      nally to make 8 triangles (I).

From the green-and-cream check, cut:
   2 squares, each 2⅞" x 2⅞". Cut once diago-
      nally to make 4 triangles (I).

From the cream-and-white print, cut:
   4 squares, each 6½" x 6½" (J)

From the medium green print, cut:
   2 strips, each 3½" x 32½" (K)
   2 strips, each 3½" x 26½" (L)

From the fabric for the binding, cut:
   4 strips, each 2" x 42"

PATCHWORK

1. Join the multicolored A rectangle and the red-and-gold check B rectangle. Add 2 bright yellow C strips to the sides, and 2 bright yellow D strips to the top and bottom edges.

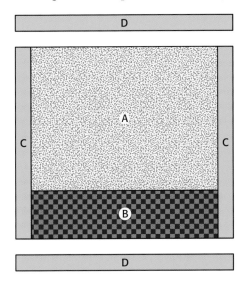

2. Join 1 white E strip to each side of the center section. Add a light gold F square to each end of the remaining 2 white E strips and attach these to the top and bottom edges.

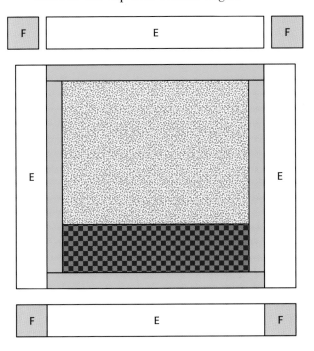

3. Join the yellow-and-green G strips to the sides and the yellow-and-green H strips to the top and bottom edges.

4. Join a white I triangle and a red-and-white I triangle to make Unit 1. Make 8 units. Join a white I triangle and a red-and-cream check I triangle to make Unit 2. Make 4 units. Join a white I triangle and a dark green I triangle to make Unit 3. Make 8 units. Join a white I triangle and a green-and-cream check I triangle to make Unit 4. Make 4 units.

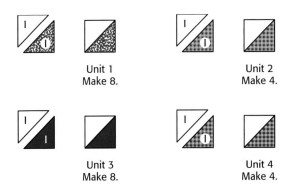

Unit 1
Make 8.

Unit 2
Make 4.

Unit 3
Make 8.

Unit 4
Make 4.

5. Join 2 of Unit 1 and 1 of Unit 2 to make each of the left and right side units. Make 2 of each. Join 4 of Unit 3 and 2 of Unit 4 to make each of the center units. Make 2.

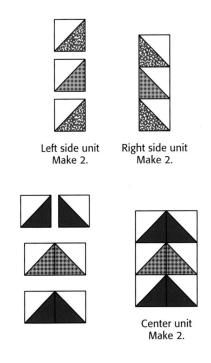

Left side unit
Make 2.

Right side unit
Make 2.

Center unit
Make 2.

6. Join a left and right side unit, a center unit, and 2 cream-and-white J squares to make each of the top and bottom sections. Add these to the top and bottom edges.

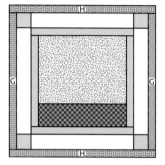

7. Add the medium green K strips to the sides of the quilt top first; then add the medium green L strips to the top and bottom edges.

APPLIQUÉ AND EMBROIDERY

Using the patterns on pages 79–82, prepare appliqué shapes following the directions for fusible appliqué on pages 9–10. Appliqué the pieces in numerical order. Appliqué the holly and berries on white E pieces after the words are embroidered.

Location	Color of Floss	Number of Strands	Stitch	Item to Embroider
Goose	Black	1	Backstitch	Outline of eye, eyelashes, line on bill
Goose	Black	1	French knot	Nostril
Goose	Black	2	Backstitch	Outline of scarf, pompon, hat brim, wing
Coins	Black	2	Backstitch	Outline of coin, number 1¢
E pieces	Black	4	Backstitch	Words
E pieces	Black	3	French knot	Dots between words

EMBROIDER THE FOLLOWING:

Make 1.

Make 2.

Make 2.

FINISHING

1. Layer the quilt top with batting and backing; baste. Quilt as desired.
2. Bind the edges of the quilt.
3. Add a sleeve, if desired.

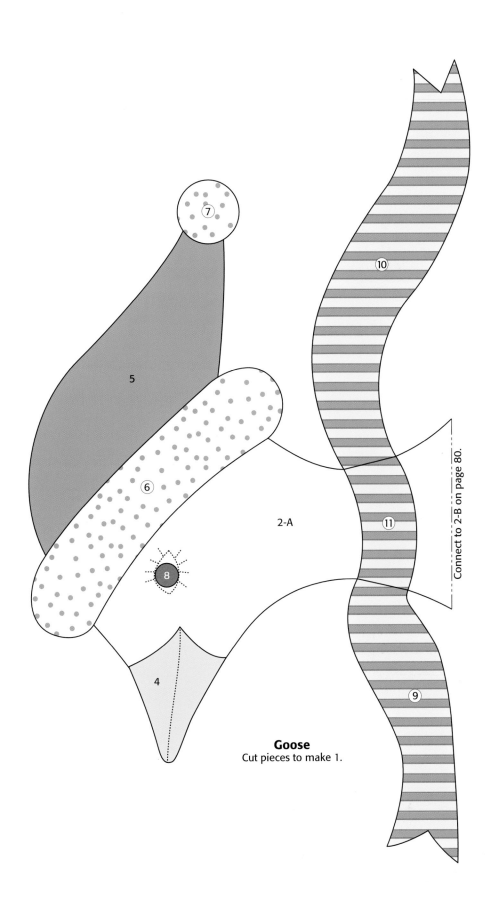

Goose
Cut pieces to make 1.

Connect to 2-B on page 80.

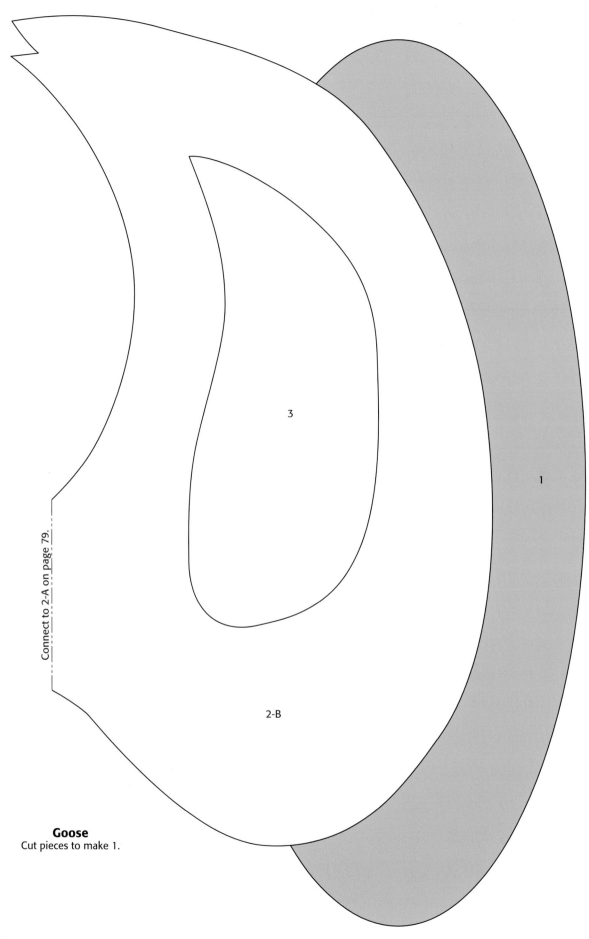

Connect to 2-A on page 79.

3

1

2-B

Goose
Cut pieces to make 1.

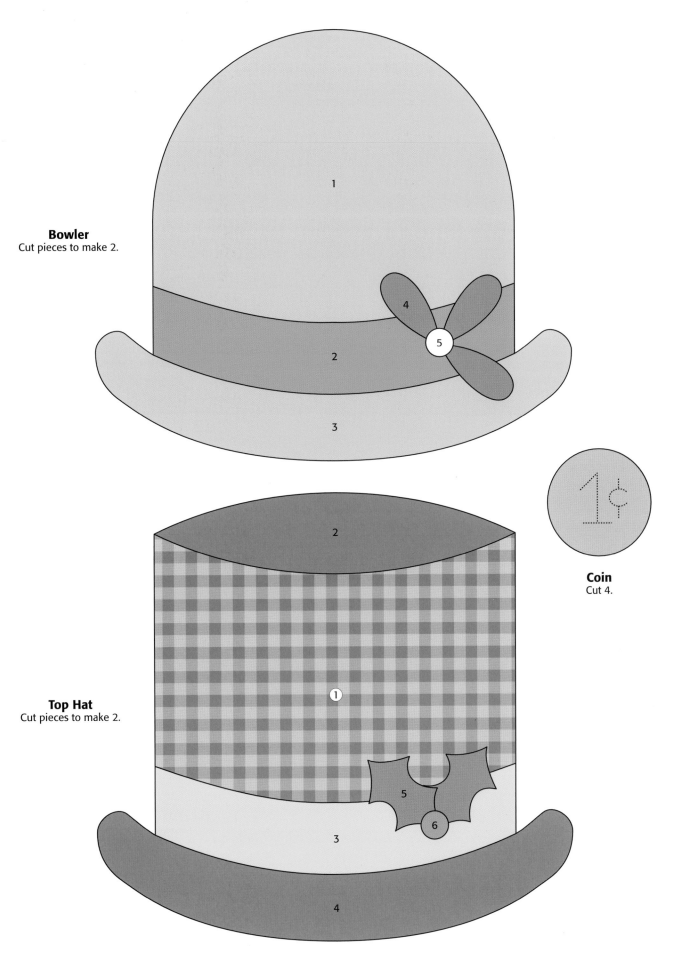

Bowler
Cut pieces to make 2.

Coin
Cut 4.

Top Hat
Cut pieces to make 2.

CHRISTMAS·IS·COMING

THE·GOOSE·IS·GETTING

FAT

PLEASE·PUT·A·PENNY·IN

AN·OLD·MAN'S·HAT

All Dolled Up for Christmas

Finished Quilt Size: 27½" x 40½"

ALL DOLLED UP FOR CHRISTMAS *by Eileen Westfall, 1999, Walnut Creek, California. Hand quilted by Donna Remorini. When I was a child and my parents would ask me what I wanted for Christmas, the answer each year was the same: "I want a doll!" I have always loved dolls and love them still. This quilt depicts three dolls that are ready for their favorite holiday.*

MATERIALS

42"-wide fabric

½ yd. white solid for background

½ yd. tone-on-tone gold print for sashing, inner border, and outer border

⅛ yd. green-and-white print for middle border

⅛ yd. red print for middle border

⅛ yd. red-and-white check for middle border

⅛ yd. multicolored print for middle border

⅜ yd. for binding

Scraps of solids and prints in the following colors for appliqué: any skin color, gold, light green, medium green, dark green, red-and-gold print, red-and-cream striped, and light brown

1 skein of embroidery floss in each of the following colors: black, red, green, gold, and a color to match the dolls' skin

31" x 45" piece of batting

1¼ yds. for backing

1 heart button

1 leaf button

CUTTING

From the white solid, cut:

    3 rectangles, each 8½" x 13½" (A)

    2 rectangles, each 3½" x 7½" (E)

    2 rectangles, each 3½" x 8½" (F)

From the tone-on-tone gold print, cut:

    4 strips, each 1½" x 13½" (B)

    2 strips, each 1½" x 28½" (C)

    8 strips, each 1½" x 3½" (D)

    2 strips, each 3½" x 21½" (H)

    2 strips, each 3½" x 40½" (I)

From the green-and-white print, cut:

    4 squares, each 3½" x 3½" (G)

From the red print, cut:

    4 squares, each 3½" x 3½" (G)

From the red-and-white check, cut:

    8 squares, each 3½" x 3½" (G)

From the multicolored print, cut:

    4 squares, each 3½" x 3½" (G)

From the fabric for the binding, cut:

    4 strips, each 2" x 42"

PATCHWORK

1. Join 3 white A rectangles and 4 gold B strips. Add the gold C strips to the top and bottom edges.

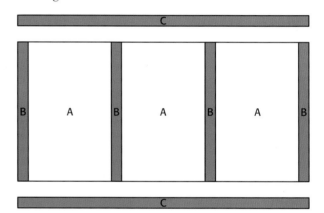

2. Join 2 red-and-white G squares, 2 gold D strips, and 1 white E rectangle to make a side border. Make 2. Join 2 gold D strips and 1 white F rectangle with 2 each of the following G squares to make each of the top and bottom borders: green-and-white, red, red-and-white, and multicolored.

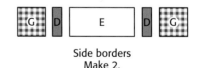

Side borders
Make 2.

Top and bottom borders
Make 2.

3. Join the side borders to the sides; then add the top and bottom borders to the top and bottom edges.

4. Add the gold H strips to the sides first; then add the gold I strips to the top and bottom edges.

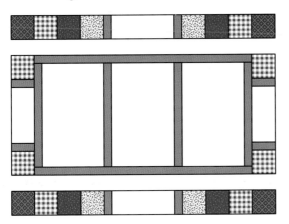

APPLIQUÉ AND EMBROIDERY

Using the patterns on pages 86–91, prepare appliqué shapes following the directions for fusible appliqué on pages 9–10. Appliqué the pieces in numerical order.

EMBROIDER THE FOLLOWING:				
Location	**Color of Floss**	**Number of Strands**	**Stitch**	**Item to Embroider**
Dolls 1, 2, 3	Black	1	Backstitch	Eyebrows, eyelashes
Dolls 1, 2, 3	Black	1	Satin stitch	Pupils
Dolls 1, 2, 3	Black	3	French knot	Nose
Dolls 1, 2, 3	Red	1	Satin stitch	Cheeks
Dolls 1, 2, 3	Red	1	Backstitch	Mouth
Doll 1	Gold	1	Backstitch	Curl, swirl in bun
Dolls 1, 2	Matching skin color	1	Satin stitch	Ears
Doll 3	Green	1	Backstitch	Brooch: stem
Doll 3	Green	1	Satin stitch	Brooch: leaves
Doll 3	Red	1	Satin stitch	Brooch: flower

Doll 1
Make 1.

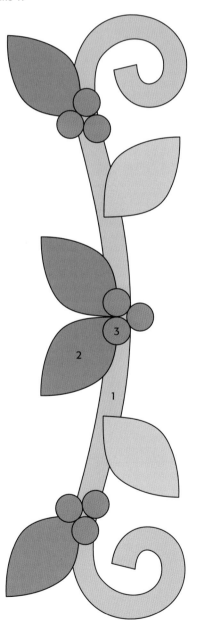

Doll 2
Make 1.

FINISHING

1. Layer the quilt top with batting and backing; baste. Quilt as desired.
2. Bind the edges of the quilt.
3. Add a sleeve, if desired.
4. Add the buttons where the collars meet on Doll 1 and Doll 2.

Doll 3
Make 1.

Block E
Make 2.

Block F
Make 2.

Short Vine
(Block E)
Cut pieces to make 2.

Long Vine
(Block F)
Cut pieces to make 2.

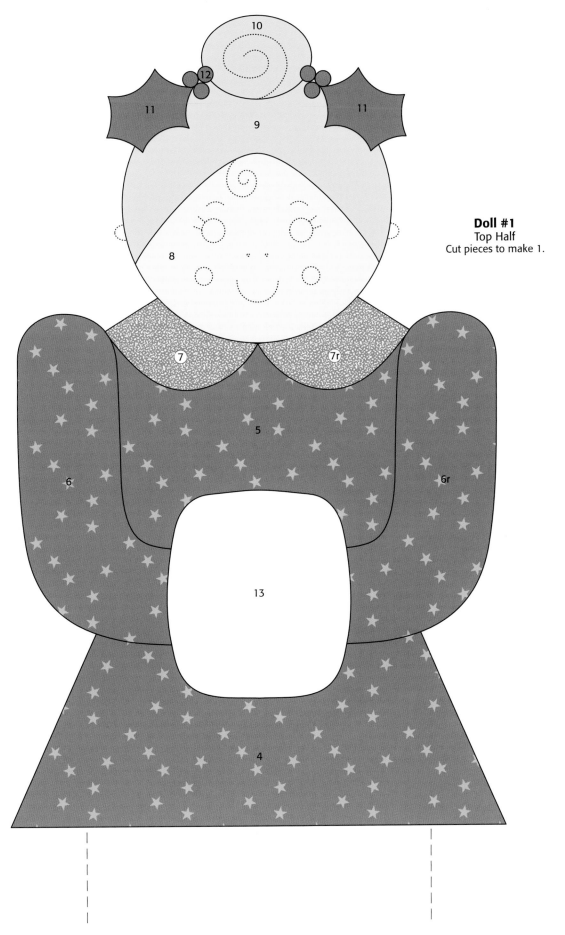

Doll #1
Top Half
Cut pieces to make 1.

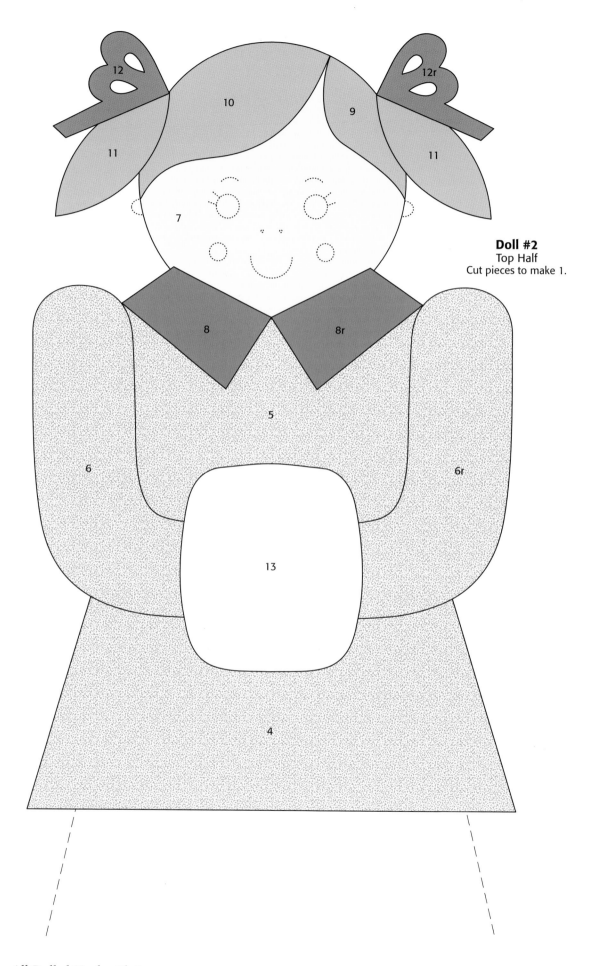

Doll #2
Top Half
Cut pieces to make 1.

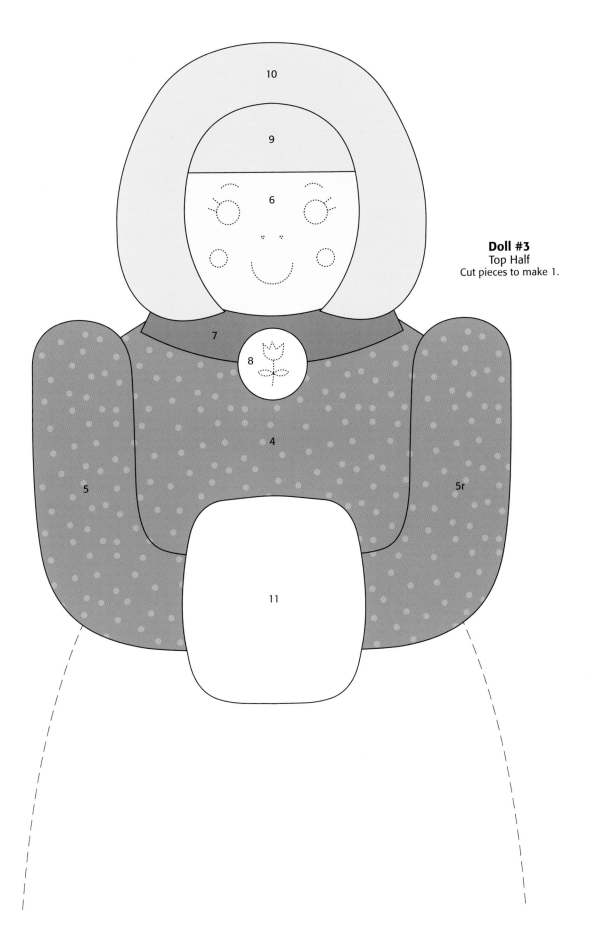

Doll #3
Top Half
Cut pieces to make 1.

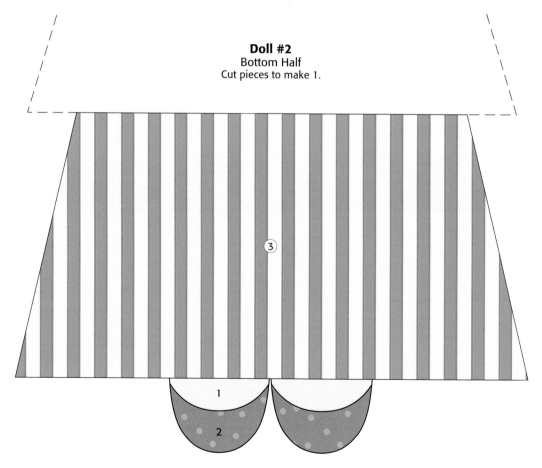

Doll #1
Bottom Half
Cut pieces to make 1.

3

1

2

Doll #2
Bottom Half
Cut pieces to make 1.

3

1

2

Doll #3
Bottom Half
Cut pieces to make 1.

Kiss Me

Finished Quilt Size: 21½" x 20½"

KISS ME by Eileen Westfall, 1999, Walnut Creek California. Hand quilted by Kim Chan. Have you ever been kissed under the mistletoe? If not, just hang this quilt in a high spot and maybe someone will get the hint! Bright candy canes, branches of mistletoe leaves, and berries surround the command "kiss me." Make this sweet quilt for someone you love.

MATERIALS

42"-wide fabric

¼ yd. light green print for inner border
¼ yd. gold fabric for background
¼ yd. white solid for middle border
¼ yd. red solid for middle border
¼ yd. red, gold, and green print for outer border
¼ yd. for binding
Scrap in solids and prints in the following colors
    for appliqué: medium green and dark green
1 skein of embroidery floss in the following
    colors: dark green and brown
24" x 24" piece of batting
¾ yd. for backing

CUTTING

From the light green print, cut:
    2 strips, each 4" x 6½" (B)
    2 strips, each 3½" x 13½" (C)

From the gold fabric, cut:
    1 square, 6½" x 6½" (A)

From the white solid, cut:
    27 squares, each 1½" x 1½" (D)

From the red solid, cut
    27 squares, each 1½" x 1½" (D)

From the multicolored print, cut:
    2 strips, each 3½" x 14½" (E)
    2 strips, each 3½" x 21½" (F)

From the fabric for the binding, cut:
    3 strips, each 2" x 42"

PATCHWORK

1. Join the 2 light green B rectangles to the sides of the gold A square. Add the light green C rectangles to the top and bottom edges.

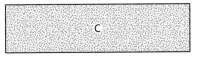

2. Join 8 white D squares and 7 red D squares to make the top border. Join 7 white D squares and 8 red D squares to make the bottom border. Join 6 white D squares and 6 red D squares to make a side border. Make 2.

Top border
Make 1.

Bottom border
Make 1.

Side borders
Make 2.

3. Add the pieced borders to the sides first; then add the top and bottom borders.

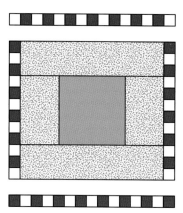

4. Add the multicolored E strips to the sides first; then add the multicolored F strips to the top and bottom edges.

Appliqué and Embroidery

Using the patterns on page 95, prepare appliqué shapes following the directions for fusible appliqué on pages 9–10. Appliqué the pieces in numerical order. Appliqué the mistletoe leaves and berries after embroidering the branches.

EMBROIDER THE FOLLOWING:				
Location	Color of Floss	Number of Strands	Stitch	Item to Embroider
Center	Dark green	4	Backstitch	Words
Center	Brown	4	Backstitch	Branches

Make 1.

Finishing

1. Layer the quilt top with batting and backing; baste. Quilt as desired.
2. Bind the edges of the quilt.
3. Add a sleeve, if desired.

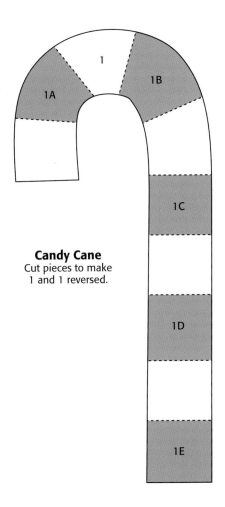

Candy Cane
Cut pieces to make
1 and 1 reversed.

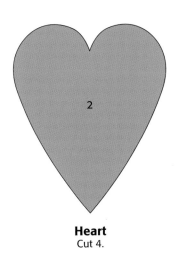

Heart
Cut 4.

KISS
ME

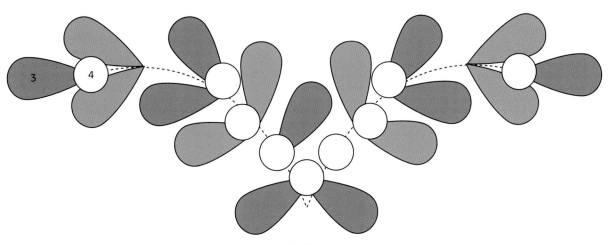

Mistletoe
Cut pieces to make 4.

About the Author

Eileen has loved quilts since she was a child and has been a quilt designer for more than twenty years. She is the author of numerous magazine articles and ten books on quilting, including *Basic Beauties: Easy Quilts for Beginners* and *Quilts Say It Best* (That Patchwork Place). Eileen lives with her husband, John, and a cocker spaniel, Josie, in a quilt-filled house in Walnut Creek, California. Eileen also has a son, Damian, who is a student at Whitworth College in Washington State.